DREAM TIME

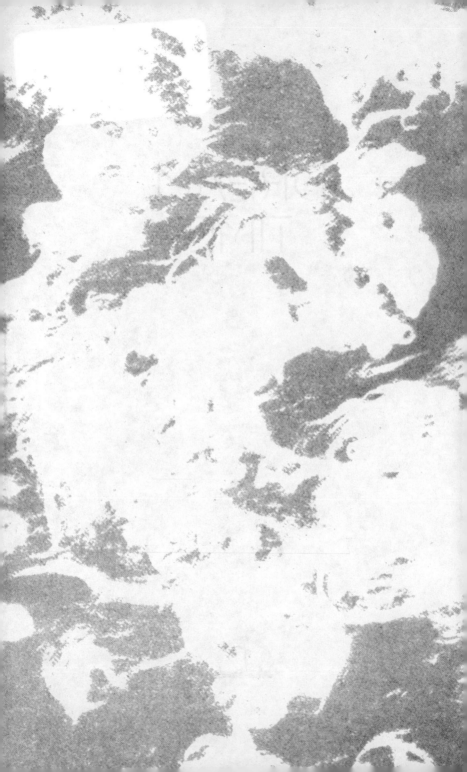

DREAM TIME

CHAPTERS FROM THE SIXTIES

GEOFFREY O'BRIEN

VIKING

VIKING
Published by the Penguin Group
Viking Penguin Inc., 40 West 23rd Street, New York, New York 10010, U.S.A.
Penguin Books Ltd, 27 Wrights Lane, London W8 5TZ, England
Penguin Books Australia Ltd, Ringwood, Victoria, Australia
Penguin Books Canada Ltd, 2801 John Street, Markham, Ontario, Canada L3R 1B4
Penguin Books (N.Z.) Ltd, 182–190 Wairau Road, Auckland 10, New Zealand

Penguin Books Ltd, Registered Offices: Harmondsworth, Middlesex, England

First published in 1988 by Viking Penguin Inc.
Published simultaneously in Canada

Portions of this book first appeared in *Telescope* magazine and *Alcatraz* magazine.

Grateful acknowledgment is made for permission to reprint excerpts
from the following copyrighted works:
"Chains" by Gerry Goffin and Carole King. © Copyright 1962 by Screen
Gems-EMI Music Inc. Used by permission. All rights reserved.
"Tupelo Honey" by Van Morrison. © 1971 WB Music Corp. & Caledonia Soul Music.
All rights reserved. Used by permission.
"The Psychedelic World" by Bernard Roseman from *LSD: The Age of Mind*.
By permission of Wilshire Book Co.
Start Your Own Religion by Timothy Leary. By permission of the author.
"Not So Sweet Martha Lorraine." Words and music by Joe McDonald. © 1969 Joyful
Wisdom Music (BMI). Used by permission. All rights reserved.
"The Word." Words and music by John Lennon and Paul McCartney. © 1965, 1967
Northern Songs Limited. All rights for the U.S., Canada and Mexico controlled and
administered by Blackwood Music Inc. under license from ATV Music (Maclen). All
rights reserved. International copyright secured. Used by permission.
"Transcendental Meditation" by Brian Wilson, Mike Love and Al Jardine.
© 1968 Sea of Tunes/Irving Music Inc.

LIBRARY OF CONGRESS CATALOGING IN PUBLICATION DATA
O'Brien, Geoffrey, 1948–
Dream time.
1. United States—Popular culture—History—20th
century. 2. United States—Civilization—1945–
3. United States—History—1961–1969. I. Title.
II. Title: Sixties.
E169.12.O24   1988   973.92   87-40434

Printed in the United States of America

Set in Plantin Light
Designed by Amy Hill

BOMC offers recordings and compact discs, cassettes
and records. For information and catalog write to
BOMR, Camp Hill, PA 17012.

CONTENTS

We are what we think,
having become what we thought.

—*The Dhammapada*

DREAM
TIME

SUBURBS

Once upon a time in the suburbs the nine-year-olds stood on the playground talking about Hiroshima. As their ice cream dripped on the asphalt they felt their way toward the enormous structures of the grown-up world. Like little adults, they huddled together exchanging serious information. The acrid fumes of a cap pistol were incense to evoke visions of blood and battle smoke and armored battalions.

"My daddy fought in Germany in the war." "My uncle has a Japanese sword." A torn flag or the loading clip from a Luger were relics of a chaos outside the playground and its blue sky. The chaos had been the world. It happened just before their memories began. On long sheets of brown paper they crayoned their imaginations of it: red and orange and yellow bursts of flame.

To their senses the school building and the driveway and the network of suburban lanes had always existed. In that unwobbling geography of rectangular lawns and sliding picture windows the seasons revolved on schedule. The death of summer was calmly succeeded by Halloween, Thanksgiving, and Christmas.

In the classroom they sat through film strips of hungry faces and diseased bodies. These were the people of other lands. The teacher once wrote on the blackboard the word *refugee* and asked: Does anybody know what this means? In the corridor it turned out that somebody's mother had been a refugee once, in Vienna, in the other world.

Among the boys on the playground—for pleasure, to educate one another, out of a sense of the fitness of things—an oral epic came into being, incorporating garbled fragments of Munich and Pearl Harbor and Stalingrad, of Rommel forced to suicide and Mussolini strung up in an Italian square. This was History, like in the *Landmark Book of Alexander the Great*, the *Golden Stamp Album of Napoleon*, or Jimmy Stewart in *The F.B.I. Story*. Everything was part of History. They would grow up and be part of it, too. It was something that happened in public, a kind of display. It was big and final. It had something to do with the awesome sleek shapes that filled the skies of *Strategic Air Command* or the arsenal of missiles poised to launch at the slightest tremor of the DEW-Line. They had seen the four-color diagrams in Junior Scholastic. Somewhere down at the end of every road of thought were the brave blue jets lined up on the runway for eventual takeoff toward dimly imagined Soviet mountains.

And that was called World War Three. It would happen, unquestionably. The label itself ordained it, because where there is a one and a two there must be a three, for completion. A child's logic is invincible.

They lived in a civilization that brought them things. They could count on a new crop of toys each Christmas, always a little more technologically advanced than last year's models: tin robots that spoke and walked, plastic rockets with a range of up to thirty feet. New television programs were provided each September to set the tone for that autumn's play, whether the props were Davy Crockett hats or Zorro capes or a rifle like Chuck Connors used. Life was to be a succession of surprise presents from the entertainment companies. With the same regularity that the world produced new snow, new tulips, or new calendar years, there would always be new games, new dress-up disguises, new launchers, and new wired tracks; new jokes, new adventure stories, exciting new designs on packages of bubble gum.

Life in the future was going to be fun, and American kids were going to have the most fun of all. There would be telephones with picture screens. People would live on the moon under bubble domes. Electronic ramps would glide noiselessly into vast siloes. Everything would be shiny and in bright colors.

The future had a style all its own. That style was foreshadowed by the glassy houses that were coming to birth around them, new gleaming homes emerging out of empty lots with their disorder of thickets and vines, out of leftover chunks of forest littered with wire and rusted cans and torn bedding. The last tangled corners were annihilated. Dawn rose on leveled ground that was now a hard-edged lawn of unvarying green, in whose exact center a clean and seamless structure had poked up.

Older houses—the ones that still predominated—were elaborate forms full of hiding places. Darkness gathered in their winding corridors and tall cupboards, basement labyrinths and tiny dormer-windowed attics. But in the new houses light was everywhere. It streamed across the patio, glistened on the chlorinated water of the aquamarine pool, lit up every corner of the airy living room. All the heavy furniture of the old architecture, the armory of plasterwork and banisters, had been flattened out and translated into broad sweeps of color, empty spaces of undefined function, rooms that seemed to open into one another. Here there was nothing to be afraid of. It was a bright world of light and space and calm water.

In the world of the old houses, no space was free of some reminder of its use. You always had to think about what you were supposed to do. But in the new houses there was space which you could make into whatever you wanted it to be. There were wide areas where you could roll back and forth and around. On the walls there were paintings that were not pictures of anything. If the old houses seemed repositories of secrets, the new houses were glass-bottomed boats in which the distinction between inside and outside began to blur. People wore swimsuits all summer and slung towels across the armless couch. When they bathed, sunlight enveloped them.

There was a succession of big green lawns. And in the sky above them hung the little dots that were Mars and Jupiter and points beyond. Space: and how passionately they longed (aged seven and nine and eleven) to go there. Somewhere out in the grown-up world the launching pads were being readied. In their lifetime men would walk on Mars. They could hardly wait.

First of all there will be the weightlessness, the ability to float within the capsule. The space vehicle's snug dimensions somehow contain freedom. Matter is lighter and you almost move beyond the body. In here you have all you need: a book to look at, a floating jug of space drink, an earphone through which distant earth sounds are piped. Out there, on the other side of the port-hole, is infinite nothingness.

Stretching their minds to try to encompass the notion of "light-year," an odd thrill shot through them. Lying in bed, they could almost imagine the lone astronaut's consciousness, enduring that nothingness—ten years, twenty years of nothingness—waiting for the rings of Saturn, or for the mouth of the time warp that would carry him into the heart of the Andromeda Galaxy.

The mere thought of intergalactic spaces could create a sensation of swimming through air. Behind closed eyelids, patterns of revolving light emerged from a black background, transforming themselves endlessly. That was a kind of sky, too. But if that was a sky, then what was the earth of that sky? It was too difficult. It was something to ask your father about in the morning, if you could remember to. Is it true that that place exists? Is it true you can be someplace else just by thinking about being someplace else? It almost seemed you could be everywhere at the same time. But then you wouldn't really exist, would you?

It was fun, it was very exciting, to have thoughts like that. Even if it was a little scary, too. You would go back to those thoughts, if you could, and feel grateful for wherever it was they were coming from.

To be able to sneak out of your own body like that was like the freedom of Aquaman to breathe underwater or of John Jones (Jahnn Jonzz), Manhunter from Mars, to become invisible or assume someone else's form. In storybooks people were always stretching and shrinking, sliding through keyholes, or finding a door hidden under a hedge and opening it and walking down the steps until the boat was reached, and the sea under the land, and the other land on the far shore of the sea.

The storybook world—an environment of water, marshland, meadow, forest, mountain—was perfect. Everything was inside it. It knew (there was a knowledge in its center) how to have the right thing happen at every turning of the road, as the ragged soldier or starving animal or terrified child moved forward into unknown land. An old woman with a tinderbox materialized because she *had* to.

Because there is a danger, insurmountable, the horror of every storybook. Death, at the hands of ogres or by imperial edict, has already been ordained. The reader of the story is a prisoner of the same law. And yet (and this is a miracle, the one and only miracle) the horror is deception, after all. Hidden in nature there is a formula, a herb, a magic packet that will dissolve it. The old woman knows. And in the end it will seem as if the only reason the giants or the bad king existed was to allow this magic packet to come into play. The world of tests and risks has been an opportunity for a charm to fulfill its role, by revealing the illusory nature of all that threatens.

In the morning of the magical act, the hero's eyes are washed clean. The real world begins: the never-to-be-chronicled eternity of his marriage to the princess.

But this, no matter how real, was not what happened now, although it had happened once and would surely somehow happen again. What happened now was more history all the time: a gangster shot dead in a barbershop, a boy's body chopped up and distributed among various suitcases, an airplane crashing into a city.

A radio voice told the time with urgency. They had never heard anybody talk like that. No matter what he said, the news man (they saw him with black mustache, gaunt cheeks, serious piercing eyes) was saying something important: this *happened*. It happened in a way that was different from the noise the crickets made outside the house. Different from the bucket of paint that was knocked over one day. It happened not just in one place but in every place, at once. It was something above them, outside them, bigger than them, happening in unseen rooms full of machines clicking.

The room with the television, after the television came, was big, and what was beyond its window—thick branches, spots of sky, sloping grassy hill—was much bigger even. As the light faded, the outside slipped away and the glowing screen in the corner became more definite and dominating. The whole room fell into darkness and the burning light inside the television silhouetted the black-and-white figures moving on the screen. The figures did not become rounder or take on color. It was more as if the room gradually got flat and monochrome.

The television was an open funnel, with its other end stuck in the middle of everything. Dots and sounds were feeding through it. One day the dots reassembled to become a newsreel of Portland, Oregon. The piercing sound was the red alert signaling the evacuation of the city. The prolonged siren had an invading effect even on television. Civil defense teams commandeered vehicles and frightened crowds pressed past the bank and the diner and the bus depot toward the city limits. That they were more of the fuzzy washed-out television figures gave them the raw appearance of being there.

At the bottom of the screen a white word flashed: SIMULATION. It flashed as they crowded the air-raid shelters and again when Portland went up in a thermonuclear cloud at the end of the program. A voice explained that it had been a necessary dramatization. The cloud at least was real, borrowed from one of the images they had already seen so many times, in a 1945 photograph or a spread in *Life* about Bikini Atoll. Later some footage from a testing ground in Utah would be spliced into the opening moments of a low-budget monster movie, where it functioned as a device to get the plot moving. It was not difficult to be aware of the Atomic Age. Everybody got the word sooner or later.

Important things usually weren't said out loud. Out loud was for the ordinary acts of passing a fork or talking about the bank or reciting a television joke. There was no tone of voice that could carry a large thing like the shape of the world. It came out as a squeak.

But things that were never said were sometimes written down in obscure places. The end of the world was announced in red letters in a four-page tract found tucked between bus seats. Line drawings of expressionless people—father, mother, child, businessman, farmer, soldier—were slotted in between prophecies in bold italics. This whisper of catastrophe came from some scary sect outside the community. It could certainly not have come from the cozy well-appointed nondenominational church by the shopping plaza, whose most extreme pamphlets tended to deal with the sexual conduct of teenagers and how to control it. Apocalypse, for that tastefully attired congregation, was precisely a pale-lipped woman in black—maybe she lived across the highway, near the truck stop, in a barely furnished shanty—thrusting the literature of terror through a suburban doorway.

There has to be, in response, a literature of comfort where you can go, whose words would affirm as durable the sunlight sweeping across hedge and patio. But the heaviest fears are sown by words that mean to reassure. The cheery red, white, and blue of a Bantam paperback called *How to Survive an Atomic Bomb* told you it was there to help you: "This fact-filled, easy-to-read book . . . will tell you how to protect yourself and your family in case of atomic attack. There is no 'scare talk' in this book. Reading it will actually make you *feel better*."

It was the tone of the doctor or dentist on the verge of inflicting pain, trying to still the patient's jerking muscles. And it never did work, no matter how calm or sonorous his voice. "There is one fact [the spokesman for the National Security Resources Board was speaking] you *must remember*—and it definitely is a *fact*. Not one person in Hiroshima or Nagasaki was killed or injured by lingering radioactivity. That is a *fact*." Thus italicized, the word "fact" itself became ominous, as if an anguished voice were screaming "Why won't you believe me?" like the witness in a Perry Mason show who always turned out to be guilty.

At school they were periodically marched into the hall, lined up, and instructed to lie down until the all clear sounded, exactly the way it said in that Bantam book: "Lie down full length on your stomach. . . . *That's the single most important safety rule in this whole book*. . . . *Everyone must always lie down full-length on his stomach with his face buried in his arms*. (Right now is the best time to practice this. Get off in your own room where you won't be laughed at and try it a few times.)" Some of the neighbors were starting to dig survival shelters in their backyards, little underground playhouses full of canned food and rifles. The rifles were for shooting the other neighbors who hadn't been smart enough to build one. The nuclear family would gather around the shortwave radio and wait. There would still be house chores to be done, and some schoolbooks so they wouldn't fall too far behind in their studies.

By now they knew that the pamphlets lied. The orderly typesetting, the stolid blocks of questions and answers were a screen to keep things from slipping through. There were so many other, more generous sources of information to fill them in on the other side of the screen. Rod Serling knew a lot more than President Eisenhower. "The Twilight Zone" was a weekly bulletin of the new, updating the earlier data of *Five* (1951), *The Day the World Ended* (1956), *World Without End* (1956), *The World, the Flesh and the Devil* (1959), or *On the Beach* (1959). If you liked to read, there were all the science fiction novels that explained things, the stories of Ray Bradbury, and the adaptations of those stories for E.C. Comics. There were even jokes about the atom bomb in *Mad*, a gallows humor commenting on its own ghastliness: "The last example of this nauseating, busted-crutch type humor is to show an atom-bomb explosion! However, this routine, we feel, is giving way to the even more hilarious picture of the hydrogen bomb!"

The jittery aftertaste of that joke clarified. It was a splinter driven through the carefully measured prose on the back of some Mentor book about Man and His Destiny. In the world of serious thought—they were just about old enough to have gotten to the edges of it—Man was always approaching the crossroads, or evaluating the long road he had traveled, or weighing his future in the balance. It never sounded so bad, especially since Man had done such remarkable things in the past. He had forged myths and symbols to express his relationship to the cosmos. He had made tools that had gotten ever more complex. He had expanded the boundaries of his mind and created a coherent body of scientific knowledge. He had written encyclopedias and dictionaries and the Great Books of the Western World, and now they were all being put on microfilm to make room for more. This Man was quite a serious character, serious enough to have invented *The Saturday Review* and *The New York Times* and long shelves of impenetrable technical journals. He was bound to find a way to squeeze out of this present dilemma. Edward R. Murrow or Albert Schweitzer or Pablo Casals would come up with something. And there would be a moment of silence at the United Nations, and then a resounding organ chorale, while sunlight streamed through the modernistic stained glass. And everywhere children of all races would gather in a ring and beam.

But in the night, lights out, Hitler and Al Capone crept up and hit Albert Schweitzer over the head. Furies were uncorked until the redeeming words of the generalizers snapped shut and ceased to exist as anything but black marks on white paper. The bed was solid and finite. It was located in a particular place. The weight of the body itself made the body shudder in the dark. The thought that "it's all *real*, throat and veins and iris," heaved up out of something that seemed to know something. As if there were a spaceman inside you.

A spaceman posted there to listen in, to gather data. A spaceman who had learned to glide through the interstices of time and space, probing for fault lines. In the remote galaxy of the coolly intelligent immortals, was an alarm going off?

At least this much was clear (who was thinking this?). The world has opened up. All the hidden caves and mountains and secret valleys are staked out, exposed. The warm dark places toward which one would have crawled, into which a whole nation of silent fugitives (guided by a rainbow or an oracle) would have crept hauling baskets and infants, are turned inside out. To be here is to be a target. Why walk into the house? Why go to the basement?

The machines have really taken over. It has already happened. Whatever horizon once existed already recoils on itself. The places constrict. Future time falters and recedes. An odor of metal interpenetrates the air molecules.

A man (they were twelve now) must have been born to do something. There must have been a book in which these things were written down. All the events, every single one, happened as though they had already been completed from the start, the way the whole tulip was in the bulb.

The tulip was in the bulb and the bulb was in the tulip and it went on like that forever. Except it didn't. It ended brutally and there was nothing. By accident.

Like a joke. By not fitting in, a joke momentarily interrupted the world. That was what made it funny. But after the joke you recognized it was a joke and went back to the integral world that the joke broke. But what if it never came back again, and the little gap stayed there and became everything?

They didn't know and they would never know. You would have to be a spaceman to know something like that. A spaceman had a different type of mind that could contain everything. It could even contain more than everything. And a spaceman didn't even have to try: that was important. A spaceman was calm and had a faintly sardonic smile, like Basil Rathbone playing Sherlock Holmes. A spaceman might be kind, but in an offhand way as if he were humoring you. Talking to you like a kid, with your trivial concept of what was real and what wasn't.

And he is not a man, really, even if he looks like Michael Rennie in *The Day the Earth Stood Still*, the benign superintelligence Klaatu with weathered face and penetrant eyes. His body itself is perhaps a force field adapting itself to human concepts. He projects images because that is all the earthlings understand. His harshness and kindness are merely ploys to manipulate the humans' behavior.

He doesn't really care about people. If they had continued to die quietly, nothing would have stirred him from his corner of the universe.

He cares only about balance. The whole thing is kept together by the balance of its parts. That's what he loves, that little oscillation when all the fields of gravity are hanging right. He can detect the smallest slackening of tension. And having detected it, he must once again ride out in the tiresome saucer, to zero in on the source of the imbalance. He had been so happy doing nothing at all. Being nothing at all, and humming at the same time. Converting energy to matter and matter to energy, back and forth, inside himself, forever. And loving it!

They had remembered all that, or invented it. It had begun to get dark. Sitting on the rug with the television glowing (the sound turned off) they had begun to forget names and years. A marble glittered at the foot of the couch by the drape, like a moon of Neptune. Now the table lamp clicked on and they were back. There was still some twilight out in the yard, enough to play by. It was a new cycle, a quicker cycle. They ran out and raced around on the grass until supper.

SPIES

In this world there was a year when all the theaters were showing movies about spies. The other half of the double bill was a farce in which people repeatedly fell on their heads, out of boats, or through glass doors. In one movie Jerry Lewis took a step backward and fell over a balcony, then came back on camera to reassure everybody it was only a joke. It was the summer after the shooting of John F. Kennedy, and Russian spies were on all the screens. In the adventure pictures they were thin, and elegantly dressed, and employed a larger vocabulary than the hero. In the comedies they were fat and balding, wore funny hats and ill-fitting coats, and fell repeatedly into canals and hotel swimming pools.

In the darkness of the movie theaters freedom stirred muddily, fumbling in the balcony or yelling at the close-up of an actor. These events occurred among emblems of order: the popcorn stand, the posters of coming attractions, the beam of the usher's flashlight, the functional divisions of space into orchestra and

14

balcony, lobby and rest rooms, aisles and seats. Minimal necessary forms preserved a frail decorum. They would hold for a little while longer. Into the murmuring dark the civilization's stories about itself unfolded.

Their subject was how to be a hero, or how to *be*. More simply, how to be a spy. How does a spy talk, wear a jacket, enter a room? Once (back in the war time) there was a small room crisscrossed by sharp-edged Teutonic shadows, in which old character actors from Hungary and Czechoslovakia and Berlin and Vienna refined their blend of incongruous accents. This was a drama of dark and light, of open spaces and enclosures. The flashlight swept across the stairwell. The shadow lunged toward the final rung of the fire escape. There was the hall to the hotel room and the man behind the door when you opened it. There was the bright street that ended, the alley that began, the figure at the far end of it with the knife under his caftan. Everything took place against an oil painting of palm trees or church spires: against the static interchangeable backdrop of "Ankara" or "Bucharest" there was a crosscutting between one large richly detailed face and another. There was a monochrome warmth.

As the days moved further and further away from the war time the dense blacks grayed, the sharp edges fuzzed. The studio backdrops were replaced by rearview projections of actual footage filmed in foreign countries. The story was still about a battle between dark and light, but more time was spent in the light, to show off the grainy stock-shot beach along which Jeff Chandler seemed to stroll.

There were still some of the old spies kicking around, soldiers of fortune, Humphrey Bogart or Robert Mitchum, hell-raisers, anarchists with hearts of gold. After the war they were largely replaced by bureaucrats: Glenn Ford or Rory Calhoun in off-the-rack mufti. The new breed of spy did not have to spend half the movie resisting the idea of enlisting in a cause; he arrived on the scene in order to enlist others. He did not have to wait for his best friend to be murdered by the bad guys. It was not immediately clear whether he had any friends. What he had was an attaché case full of coded address lists, transcripts of conferences on weaponry, data on Communist penetration of foreign labor movements.

This human machine had a certain neutered charmlessness. The producers teamed him up with European starlets or bouncy second-string contract actresses, but the spark did not ignite. When Yvonne de Carlo or Luana Patten tried to seduce this button-down Sir Galahad, he responded with a prim little lecture about Soviet domination. The government agent walked stiffly through the fleshpots of Frankfurt and Bangkok and Buenos Aires, indifferent to temptation, as sealed off—like an air-conditioned room—to exotic loveplay as to exotic ideology.

But the black-and-white world transmutes into color and the spy changes again. In order to be worthy of 1964—a year that seeks out airy freshness with the obsessive determination of a fetishist—the war of light and shadow must be transformed into the multihued, morally neutral metamorphoses of a kaleidoscope.

When its electronic patterns are rendered in blue and pink, even a radar screen becomes sensual. And outside the camouflaged missile research center the camera tracks back to show the actual soil and air and vegetation of Kingston or Biarritz. The spy is no longer in front of but in the *midst* of all this. A new, *dense* world is revealed, a world of multiple levels: we have all become complex together! The primitive spy movie could sustain at best one double cross. The form evolves toward an increasingly impenetrable interlacing of false identities: people in disguise, agencies in disguise, nations in disguise. Even time can be disguised: in *36 Hours* the Nazis went to work on James Garner and convinced him (by dyeing his hair gray, printing false newspapers, hoisting an American flag over a German hospital compound, etc.) that it was really 1954 and the war had been over for years. Such a device seemed to partake of an elaborate aestheticism. No one had ever imagined such a wonderful game before.

The formalization of the espionage melodrama codified the transition from the spy who was a courageous fighter for justice to the spy who played an abstract, nihilistic game. The revelation of the spy's cynicism was like a sexual liberation. Just as the pleasure of sex could be intensified (as people were now suggesting) by being freed of any link to devotion, likewise delight in espionage fantasies was stimulated by the absence of notions of good and evil. The deletion of moral values increased the number of possible plot permutations. George Nader, operations director of an unnamed U.S. agency, might even turn out not to be the hero. And as for the European girl—who by 1958 had removed her bra just beyond the frame (it dropped obligingly into camera range) and by 1964 removed it on screen, but with her back to the camera—her loyalties were anyone's guess.

The study of spies was by now a universal vocation. While the parent sat on the couch reading (as a respite from the political analyses of *Time* or *U.S. News & World Report*) *The Spy Who Came In from the Cold* or *The Ipcress File*, the child went out to see *From Russia with Love*, came home to watch "I Spy" or "Mission Impossible" while leafing through *Nick Fury, Agent of SHIELD*, and in a moment would switch on the radio and hear Johnny Rivers singing "Secret Agent Man." The child sensed that this spy business was more than a continuation of the adventures of Doc Savage or Batman; it was a new way of talking about the world, or more precisely a way of talking about the new world.

If he asked a question—but he didn't—it might have been: What is a spy?

No answer. (A wonderful silence.) It is impossible to define the spy's identity. (A superb zero.) That's the difference between the spy and other people. Everything about the spy is outward. Inside there is nothing, not even a hole. His being is wholly absorbed in the smooth *whoosh* of hotel elevators, the tailoring of Italian jackets, methodologies of seduction and interrogation. Ancient brandies and miniaturized stilettos: anything that pierces. All these material things—foods, weapons, rooms, bodies—he monitors and manipulates. His movement around and between their fissures is a dance, and that dance is as much of an identity as he will ever have. The most dishonorable of heroes murders with a dart in the nape of the neck and sleeps with his best friend's wife in order to run a security check. The mark this leaves on him is not shame but rather the wistfulness of the spy, his self-indulgent rueful irony, an emotional trademark that endears him to serious dark-haired women in Brussels and Milan. They are attracted to the way he embodies a dandified alienation. There are a few hours to kill before the next telephone call. A fine rain continues to fall in the capital city; there is, significantly, a meaningless close-up of swans or sparrows fluttering in the drizzle. Their only respite from the hermetic universe of institutionalized terror is afternoon sex and coffee and the music of Corelli. She has a pet cat, which will, of course, be eviscerated by the KGB. And then she will turn out to be one of Their agents, recruited—once again—by his own side's Director of Operations.

Their brains are maps. Under hypnosis they recapitulate underground fuel transport systems and the orbital patterns of satellites. Their job is to understand the machines, and so they have become machines. Somehow that makes them sexy. It takes willowy grace to slide a hypodermic under someone's kneecap and then disappear, with an airy feinting movement, into the background chatter of the diplomatic reception. Later they walk—each separately—on the crowded bourgeois avenue like any other tourists, their trajectory punctuated by staccato bursts of oboe and electric guitar. Their life is rhythmically ordered and as perfectly void as a chess game. They glide through space and time, cool and razor-sharp and deeply sensitive to physical surfaces. Their life is grounded in awareness of texture. They are looking for the whorl of dust lying where no air current could have blown it.

In their few spare moments, at the Athens Hilton or along an obscure stretch of Spanish coastline, they enjoy highly condensed fun. They have no time for the preliminaries and evasions of the others (or, as these know them, the spied-on). At any moment the elevator door may spring open, or the marksman in the helicopter strafe their balcony. In this realm of permanent danger their senses are heightened. The burgundy and the satin and the kiss are luminous openings like a nave or the core of a prayer. It is a voluntary suspension of the rules that define their world. They need this union—the two beautiful spies preparing to betray each other—and in the brief blinding orgasm they are cleared of the memorized scenarios and organization charts. In that privileged space they are permitted to spy on each other's spying in a medium that does not require the divulging of actual codes.

But you, luxuriating viewer, are likewise allowed a peek, spying on them as they spy on their spying. The privilege is a corollary of democracy. In the sealed-up states of the East there are slate-gray fortresses whose exteriors are devoid of content. The air is silent and unchanging. Meanwhile, on the bare screens of the West, there are continual brief weddings of data and expressive form, bouncing off each other like electrons. How store and analyze all the facts about even a few hours of television viewing: the marketing strategies revealed by a new dog food commercial, the crucial details visible to experts in the footage of a press conference, the relevant information slipping past a drunken starlet's lips on "The Joey Bishop Show," the ingestion of a controlled substance deducible from the newscaster's enlarged pupils?

The masters of this world are capturing information, storing it, sifting it, integrating files, and cross-indexing salient characteristics. Input is hard to discard. The gum wrapper someone dropped on the boardwalk might be important. The intelligence agency's ultimate intent is the processing of *all* data, relevant or not, relevance being an eely and unreliable element of the equation Knowledge = Power. This processing is a matter, not of heroism or intelligence, but chiefly of having access to the best equipment that unlimited secret funding can buy.

If you could see what the spy sees you would quickly become dizzy. The vertigo of Nick Fury or James Bond falling from a helicopter toward an atomic island is a crude symbol of what you'd feel could you once see the web laid bare: the writhing intertwining unity of all the secret transactions of which the world is built. This is the hermetic science, the modern alchemy that links Swiss financiers and South African mining engineers and strategists in Langley, Virginia; Romanian bacteriologists and Lebanese real estate developers and Central African generals obsessed with militarism and ritual murder. From the Madison Avenue artisan designing the logo to be intaglioed on a mauve bar of soap to the Jakartan functionary establishing a file on the sexual proclivities of visiting diplomats, all are joined in the common dance. Every hand holding its little rubber stamp, every finger pressing a button to admit an outside party to secure premises: each sends out shock waves to whose collective rhythm the world structure is vibrating.

The world that was (continuity of grassland in which a horse pounded, or sea swell bearing up a wooden boat, an existence in which there might be more than minor significance in a man walking down a road or flexing a bare arm) has been renovated down to its roots. The visible stuff is still visible—the road, the arm, the meadow, the fly on the cow's tail—but as ornament, a concession to persistent ancient ideas of ceremonial fitness. Cheap tin humans dangle on the world's real body, which is electronic. From end to end, along its fault lines, it's wired. Impulses respond to impulses. Somewhere deep in the big structures, below ground level, generals at long tables study printouts of sonar readings. One particular spurt of blips flattening and intensifying might be the wedge that will pry open the self-monitoring, electronically sealed gates of the final launching.

Try to imagine those generals: this became one of the games of the day. People read *Fail-Safe* and *Seven Days in May*. They wanted to enter the government mind, hear its secrets, intuit the physical sensations of, say, a president drinking coffee. The imagination could not make him big enough. The huge brain and muscles and will of the leader could not, somehow, survive this probe. The man in the conference room was too tiny to hold up the world; only just big enough to let everything slide.

A year before the shooting of John F. Kennedy, for instance, on a warm autumn evening the President preempted regular television programming to give advance notice of the possible erasure of the world. On the street the neon was just coming on. People were walking around in the usual way. Never had ordinary gestures—buying a newspaper, putting the key in the lock, shoving a quarter across the counter, waiting on line to see the new adventure movie—seemed so submissive, so humiliated. The people on the street had in any case no way of responding. Even if a more precise hour were fixed for the great dissolution, the hand would continue in automaton fashion to shove the coin across the counter. The fingers might tap more or less rapidly, the tempo of breath undergo strange and sudden changes, the dorsal configuration slump forward or arch back violently. But there would certainly not be time enough to learn a new way to move in one's body or to invent a language in which it might be possible to say something at such a moment. There would not be time enough to learn the proper way to behave.

So, by default—staring however briefly into the burning face of reality—we would retain the manners of a casual bystander, a member of the audience. No one would guess how much this concerns us, any more than they could imagine, from his air of polite boredom at the technical conference, the fiercely concentrated attention of the trained spy.

GLAMOUR

When Kennedy took over the airwaves to talk about global strategy, he committed an intrusion. At that very moment the evening paper proclaimed: LIZ FLIES TO DICK IN ROME. Just before the variety show was interrupted by military bulletins, the audience had been focused on a silvery jet streaking toward Cinecitta and the shambles of *Cleopatra*: a bright wreckage full of heat and color. Somewhere in there a Technicolor blood offering was being readied, a spectacle pulsing with erotic nuance as compared with the generic flatness of the political address. Even the President—even, when it came down to business, *this* President—was little more than the teacher standing in front of the blackboard, using phrases—"farm price supports" or "proportional representation"—that would be multiple choice answers in current events class. To be more than that—to be fully human and to have one's flesh sincerely loved—would require crossing over into the sacral realm of the screen stars.

The world of government consists of rectilinear boxes hierar-chically arranged. The figure in the niche—Secretary of State or Agriculture, Director of Central Intelligence—is essentially devoid of personality traits. He functions as part of the machinery that makes things go, like the remote sources of energy powering the lights and the refrigerator. If they stop, it all stops; but beyond that there is no question of *liking* them.

Usually there is not even a question of thinking about them. News programs end early. Afterward the mind is free to imagine a world of intimate and endlessly fascinating adult behavior, in which bureaucrats play no part. That world is about passion, betrayal, jealousy, infatuation, all the truths of heart and groin that the movie stars were born to mirror. The stars come into existence unpredictably; none knows in what cradle the next will be found. They arise as if to redress an obscure imbalance, to fulfill a longing indefinable until their presence gives it a name. They have come to provide a language of bodies. Each—Marilyn Monroe, Marlon Brando, James Dean, Kim Novak, Steve McQueen, Shirley MacLaine—is a world, a culture, a repository of dialects and gestures. They offer something better than words or ideas: an absolute particularity. The cadence of a retort or the way bone structure is revealed in an abrupt grimace is unique. Nobody smiles like Lee Remick; nobody has a forehead quite the same as Paul Newman's. The politicians, being interchangeable, say and do the same things over and over. It's the stars who bring change into the world.

James Dean invented his own hair, his own jacket, his own death. Marlon Brando taught people new ways to speak and move their bodies. Marilyn Monroe opened up new areas of the world at each step, moving like an explorer through unexplored jungles of public desire. Her death would later be felt as the first of a string of public deaths. Inevitably it would be woven into the web of conspiracy theory that embodied the collective intellectual process of the time. The light of beauty—that bubbly smile—could hardly be extinguished without a cause. Her sudden disappearance in midsummer was like a premonition of further loss.

But movies must be made, new stars must go on in place of the dead. The screen must be filled, even if Rod Taylor or Pamela Tiffin lack the soul-stirring depth of the ancestral stars. Gable is gone, Coop is gone, Marilyn is gone, Jimmy Dean is gone. In their absence we find ourselves switching over to a different mode of spectacle, a farce of passions like this complex net of Debbie and Eddie and Liz and Dick and Sybil. Like all the best public shows, it can be read in a number of ways: as squalid domestic drama, as morality play of scarlet woman and jaded foreigner, or—more aptly, as it transpires—as the acting out of a tidal change in sexual conduct, a Europeanization of mores long desired in secret.

And what more appropriate occasion than the opulent catastrophe of *Cleopatra*? The squandering of millions on an epic that nobody wanted to see was itself the epic that people wanted to see. The spirit of gaudy prodigality reigning over the production mingled with the aphrodisiac trappings of an imagined Rome: the Rome of *La Dolce Vita* (which had recently introduced the concept of "foreign movies" to a vast new audience) translated into the Rome of Vincente Minnelli's *Two Weeks in Another Town*, with starlets leaping naked into fountains and Kirk Douglas stalking Cyd Charisse through mirrored rooms crowded with hashish-smoking sophisticates. The vision of America as a hell of domestic dead ends, played out sullenly against a backdrop of roadhouses and auto showrooms, could now be abandoned for a more attractive hell in which everybody wore sunglasses, spoke several languages, practiced elaborate sexual perversions, and took pride in a knowledge of brandies. Silver-haired sybarites manifested a refined world-weariness in the form of enigmatic hand gestures. Italy was a spiritual center, creating for the twentieth century not Dante or Giotto but a philosophy embodied in cosmetics and footwear and futuristic furniture design.

Presiding over this shift in manners was the Janus-headed John F. Kennedy. While in one aspect of his being he was unleashing military "advisers" in Vietnam and the CIA at the Bay of Pigs, in another he was simultaneously exemplifying the newborn American version of hedonism, consorting with movie actresses and playfully manipulating the erotic shadings of his own public image, as if to say: "I am what you want to be." His favorite spy, James Bond, became the universal favorite; if the average man could not drink the President's burgundies or sleep with his mistresses, he could at least afford to read the same pulp fiction. Kennedy smiled on his glorification by the media, which encompassed his portrayal by Cliff Robertson in *PT 109* and his identification with King Arthur in connection with the musical *Camelot*, starring—who else?—Richard Burton.

Yet if antique metaphors were to be bandied, surely ancient Rome would have been more suitable than the Round Table. While dispatching shock troops to shore up the defenses of the outer provinces, the President cultivated a suggestion of orgiastic ebullience at the empire's heart. He even made a show of gathering artists and intellectuals around him like so many Ciceros or Ovids. One could picture an elite as brilliantly articulate as Laurence Olivier and Charles Laughton and Peter Ustinov in Stanley Kubrick's recently released *Spartacus*.

For the moment the Corn Belt moralizers, the homespun Norman Rockwell Republicans who had loomed so tall in the committee hearings of the fifties, were cast in a ludicrous light. The gawky figure in specs and waistcoat could now be transformed into a stereotype of the nation's secret shame: the sexual clumsiness of the American male. Each time a European actress (to whom the newly fashionable word "sensuous" was invariably applied) gave an interview, she would harp on the same theme. The American male was rigid, unadventurous, insensitive to the needs of women, condemned by a self-torturing Puritanism to an inability to "let go." Only President Kennedy suggested the possibility of an American lover capable of competing with Alain Delon or Marcello Mastroianni. But now that Jack stood in front of the map of Cuba, offering neither a boyish grin nor an insouciant toss of that wavy hair, the fear hit. Had we waited too long? Would there not, after all, be time for the enormous party just beginning to be imagined?

His assassination the following autumn seemed to stimulate the new era of fun, providing the note of desperation that flavors the wildest parties. Now there could never be enough toys. There certainly could never be enough time to play with them all. By 1966 future filmmakers David Newman and Robert Benton would be whimsically suggesting in the pages of *Esquire* that the rest of the decade be canceled, enough having already happened. Side by side with a photograph of Andy Warhol and Nico dressed as Batman and Robin, the authors offered their catalog of sixties paraphernalia: "Vinyl fashions . . . surfing . . . underground movies . . . the Zip Code which nobody uses . . . Op Art . . . the kidnapping of Frank Sinatra Jr. . . . electric toothbrushes . . . Diet-Cola . . . *Eros* . . . Super-8 . . . topless bathing suits . . . charcoal-filter cigarettes."

Outside the Riviera Café on Sixth Avenue a sign was posted: SCOPITONE IS HERE. On the television screen above the jukebox a ghostly image of Sylvie Vartan in a miniskirt sang "Twiste et Chante." Sybil Burton's discotheque Arthur, for a moment the hottest in New York, was likewise full of miniskirts. Miniskirts were new. Everything was new: white boots, thickly mascaraed eyes proclaiming their own artifice, the long undulant hair of Samantha Eggar or Susannah York. *Time* paid tribute to "London: the Swinging City." A new genre of festivity appeared to be taking shape.

It was as though the private fun of the rich was spilling over into the public domain. Even pornography—an aristocratic prerogative under the Ancien Régime or in Victorian England—was to be made available to the democratic masses. In the process a quiet change took place. The boring old liberal argument that "*Lady Chatterley's Lover* is not obscene but rather a deeply felt, profoundly humanistic work of art" gave ground to the awareness that *Lady Chatterley* really was pretty heavy-handed and old-fashioned, whereas there was much more fun to be had with *Candy* or *Fanny Hill* or such pseudonymous authors of the Traveller's Companion Series as Akbar del Piombo or Harriet Daimler. "Eroticism" was the magic word. A gate opened. Many had been waiting.

The debate continued, of course, especially in terribly serious magazines such as *Encounter* (nobody knew it was a CIA front yet) and *The Atlantic Monthly*, but by now other voices were ready to counter that the trial was over and there was no need to placate anybody with specious arguments about "socially redeeming values." Yet even within this reformulated stance the eternal war of Europe and America continued, in which the native aesthetic of the carnival midway, the peep show, the dirty comic book was pitted against Old World sexual rituals of forbiddingly hieratic elegance. America came forth with the works of, say, Orrie Hitt (*Trailer Tramp, Ex-Virgin, Lust Prowl*) and Europe responded with *The Story of O* or *Our Lady of the Flowers*. While the Americans remained obsessed with good and evil, innocent and corrupt, clean and dirty, the Europeans explored with mandarin detachment the dialectic of pain and pleasure, dominance and submission, restraint and abandon.

The Americans—or more specifically the American men for whom sleazy publishers had fashioned novels such as *Bayou Girl, Convention Girl, Gutter Girl, Marijuana Girl*—dwelt obsessively on a single image of despoiled innocence. Joy did not enter into their fantasies; there was simply the brute fact of a cheerleader's loss of virginity, as if love had died there. These were the secret testimonials of a shame culture, the expiatory texts of a male society uncomfortable with its need to sully a purity it somehow depended on. The fathers had made that purity the cornerstone of their moral world—why then should they want to see it transformed into a lewdness and depravity almost beyond their imagination?

As if to heal this fissure, the erotic came out into the open. Not only were all the nasty secrets to be aired, they were in the process to be cleansed and transformed. The reassuring message would be: "Don't worry! It's all right!" Step by painful step, permission was granted. Middle-class couples who would scarcely have ventured into a Forty-second Street grindhouse to see *Surfside Sex* or *Orgy at Lil's Place* could allow themselves to enter a spanking new Upper East Side cinema (aromatic with espresso) for a screening of *I, a Woman*. Making love in the tall grass, in Swedish, was both clean and artistic. (At mid-decade the Swedish blonde was, along with the liberated airline stewardess, the primary sexual icon.) Concealed nudities awaited the imminent crumbling of barriers, while eyes rehearsed the frank and unashamed gaze appropriate for future unveilings. Best-selling paperbacks coyly explained the stylistics of fellatio. Television comedians made oblique references to contraceptives. The single word "foreplay" engendered a thousand magazine articles, while at the same time the too brutal "climax" was replaced by the more tonally pleasurable "orgasm." A hygienic sexuality emerged, gliding as smoothly as the camera movements in a soap commercial. Its totem was the Pill, enshrined on the cover of *Time* as an iconic lozenge beaming like a crucifix in a rose window. The hour of free love was at hand. America, having already emerged from provincialism in the arts and in international politics, would accede to maturity in the bedroom. Relief and anticipation shot through the society.

The new sense of freedom, as it spread, led into a contagious case of the giggles. The gaiety, the champagne-piquant frivolity that had been part of the Kennedy style lived on, changing (as if unmoored by his death) into hysterical light-headedness. Around this time, movie critics started talking about a golden age of film comedy: a curious judgment to pass on a cycle of movies that aimed at frothy exuberance but were closer to the half-giddy, half-sickened disjointedness of a bunch of compulsive partygoers beginning to run out of steam. *The Pink Panther*; *A Shot in the Dark*; *Kiss Me Stupid*; *The Patsy*; *The World of Henry Orient*; *What's New, Pussycat?*; *Lord Love a Duck*; *The Swinger*; *Don't Make Waves*; *Caprice*: they all shared an edgy failure to sustain any emotional note for long. Sudden changes of mood, hard-edged farce abruptly giving way to a sort of hung-over tenderness, carefully established character relationships dissolving in elephantine pratfalls. It was all very modern: jagged and permanently out of kilter.

There were parties. There would be more and more of them. In 1968, when Blake Edwards sought to epitomize his farceur's craft, what title could he choose but *The Party*? What else had been going on? Once people gave parties to celebrate their achievements; now they achieved things in order to give parties. Fun had never been more serious. The party was not a respite but the goal itself, the ultimate field of action. The permanent crisis of the

modern world had proven too wearing. People needed an intermission. For the moment they didn't want a new philosophy or
a new political system, only a new design for sunglasses, a new
way of half-revealing young thighs, a new way of lighting a room
to accentuate that revelation. To be flashy and madcap was to
perpetuate a religion of the fleeting instant. Preternaturally thin
models sported metal and plastic amid the neon tubing and shim-
mering canvases of the galleries, Andy Warhol dined with Kennedy's widow, men in tuxedos danced what they called the frug,
the Museum of Modern Art displayed modular Italian furniture,
and even on Times Square another Italian import (Antonio Margh-
eriti's *Wild, Wild Planet*) announced that the future had already
arrived: astronauts in vinyl engaged in somnambulistic go-go dancing
with girls in purple makeup and microskirts, in the disco lounge
of a spaceship, to the beat of interestingly simplistic computer
music.

When the future spoke—as it did every day now—it spoke
through jukeboxes. In the paradise of affluence Dionne Warwick
was always singing a Burt Bacharach song, as a Greek island came
into view at starboard. The stars—movie actresses, pop singers,
grizzled dissipated novelists, intellectual fashion designers—got
hilariously drunk in ship's bars, alternately fell half-naked down
casino steps or announced their intention of filming the work of
Genet or Ouspensky. The planet was their plaything. Having the
power of free movement to and from anywhere, they jetted between Corfu and Bhutan and the Seychelles, colliding briefly with
one another to invent new psychic spaces, to share the new fun
of the incandescent future.

From time to time they acted in movies, sang songs on records
or television, were photographed entering restaurants. But these
were mere outward signs. The point, the heart, was elsewhere:
in the private lives of the celebrities, deep in the whorl of endlessly

ramified interconnections they were creating among themselves. They mated and split, bonded and dispersed as if to illustrate the principals of physics. Adorably they embodied fluctuation. Their function was to be mercurial, to provide the constant movement and stimulation that kept the show alive. It took a lot of energy to keep that dazzle going. A few fell down on the job, but that was part of the pattern. Some of the most exciting scenes depicted the violent disintegration of a star letting himself go.

They were no longer stars of the old mold, fat contented golfers surrounded by bodyguards in their Las Vegas suites. These new ones had something more than money to expend: their lives. They would spill themselves out, offering themselves as sacrifice to sustain the gigantic international coproduction that was the temporal world. The history of the decade was to be a sequence of recognized faces, floodlit, televised, polarized, framed by the borders of a magazine cover or by the wall to which a poster was affixed. We knew each of them intimately: drunk, terrified, seductive. The anguish of the star—his scars, his mirrors, his splintered self—was the theme of a public ritual. The solitary hero crashes into the world. The beautiful enchanter is whirled into pieces within her own enchantment. They were so big even when they fell. Pictures of the lips and ears and knees were wrapped in cellophane and sold. They talked. They sat in a chair. They blinked the bloodshot eyes and lit another cigarette. They were so vast that we could almost live comfortably in their reflected light.

THE PARADISE OF BOURGEOIS TEENAGERS

In adolescence all the novels came to life. Bad Girl, a silhouette in black leather, leaned against the chain-link. Dusk was coming on through the twisty downtown streets. The low-budget neon of the cigar store and the laundromat glowed on her as she tilted the Viceroy up to her candy-apple lips. From the far end of the playground Johnny Boy hooted something like "Those boots are boss, chick!" The vinyl tips shimmered in the half-light. Bad Girl's high laugh cut like a stiletto across the asphalt: "Which Frankie Avalon picture is that from, Johnny?" Johnny Boy shambled and mugged, cupped his hands to light a Lucky in the wind, and sidled up to her with what he took to be catlike grace. Smokey Robinson's falsetto drifted by on somebody's car radio.

They were pacing out the margins of their neighborhoods. One by one they mapped obscure entrances, stained steps descending from street level toward exotic basements, a few legendary park benches ("He's there every Friday late evening"), shops with misleading names, alleys where people gathered surreptitiously to *connect*. The playground was a rendezvous point near the raw edge: "Who are we waiting on?" "The Kid is meeting his dealer on MacDougal Street. He'll signal us from the corner and then we'll go up to his parents' crib and get high." "Hey, that sounds out of sight." "You ever blow boo, Johnny?" "Sure, that's all I do." "Which imitation are you doing now?" "James Dean in *Rebel Without a Cause* when Corey Allen asks him if he's ever been on a chicken run."

Johnny Boy should have been at home practicing the violin—he was so good at it—and Bad Girl had been forbidden ever to go near MacDougal Street again. There had already been trouble. In theory she had gone, tonight, to the Filmmakers' Cinémathèque for the Kenneth Anger retrospective. Her parents had of course never seen *Scorpio Rising* or *Inauguration of the Pleasure Dome*, but she informed them that Anger was "a leading surrealist film artist" and they gave grudging consent. She had already seen the Anger films anyway, so there was no problem there. She had even met Jonas Mekas after the screening, and he had asked her what her generation thought about Vietnam; she thought he was really spiritual, really crazy. Johnny Boy was jealous in silence and wanted to say: Don't let those bohemians cart you off to some orgy.

Meanwhile the Kid had materialized on the street corner, looking a little like Corey Allen in *Rebel Without a Cause*, a little like Bob Dylan on the cover of his second album—the one where he was walking along Bleecker Street with a "soulful-looking chick." (So many people had thought about her, wondered who she was, tried to imagine what her thoughts were like.) The Kid was a great source of practical information. He knew all about where to "cop" (the word was relatively new to them) and how to spill the first taste of wine on the floor "for the boys upstate." The Kid even knew Dylan slightly, or had been in the same room with him—or perhaps it had been a friend of the Kid's. Even so there was a sort of pedigree of authenticity in having *friends* like that, just as there was in being able to manage a deft palm slap at the signal of "Give me five, bro," to be conversant in jailhouse slang, or to know the right store to buy boots at: not the gaudy one on Eighth Street itself but the hidden one three streets away where they are more beat-up looking. You have to know these things.

The world around them was the Village. It had always been there, but now they were old enough to understand that it was the fountain of knowledge. Within its doorways and attics, behind its hand carved shutters, lived the agents of an invisible world: poets, bebop saxophonists, actors, civil rights lawyers, junkies, homosexuals, historians of anarchism. A man in Japanese sandals and a Japanese robe sits on a bamboo mat naked to the waist playing a long and seemingly formless solo on a bamboo flute. Sandals, robe, mat, and flute were souvenirs of his Okinawa tour of duty. That must have been around the time he started smoking reefers. On the next landing the white-haired man who knows all about James Joyce and Kabbalistic lore shares youthful memories of Aleister Crowley and Nancy Cunard with the lesbian novelist across the hall, she having taken a tea break from her multivolumed novel on memory and desire, now thirty years in the writing. Down the block the two retired Communists break off their chess game to debate, again, the Bukharin question. Old free people—from the twenties! a legendary breed—enjoy silk screens and Renaissance music and civilized orgies within curtained precincts. It is a city within a city.

On the avenue the leather jackets line up outside the pizza parlor. There are transactions in the park. Police officers converge on the unlicensed bongo player. Marijuana is sold at the kitchen entrance of the folk music club. The Italian restaurant with the green curtains caters to homosexuals. The church theater announces a tribute to disarmament, while on the steps a crazed woman passes out a mimeographed leaflet about brainwashing and electrodes. Shrubs flower in the cobblestoned alley. The genuine Italian coffee leads to discussions of Schopenhauer and Lester Young. Three doors down they are showing *Rashomon* again. It is a movie about the relativity of truth. Washington Irving once lived near where the peace center is. Or that's what somebody told me.

People lucky enough to have apartments on the blocks with trees have lived there a long time. On the bookshelf the works of Kropotkin and Sherwood Anderson, by the record player a pile of 78s: Paul Robeson, Don Byas, Art Tatum, Segovia. Pussy willows jut from the earthenware jug bought in Taos. Memories of Florence and Harlem are exchanged over chianti. They still come out on the street to gather signatures against the Bomb.

Somewhere nearby, sequestered on one of the warehouse blocks, is the narrow loft—smoky, dilapidated, the wine-stained mattresses deployed randomly on the floorboards—at whose far end a small combo plays interminable moody jazz as the long afternoon fades into evening. A gaunt man in dark glasses, capable of frenetic flailing gestures, grabs a mike and initiates a verbal chant, an instant poem: "To improvise is to invent heaven." He talks about sex and outer space and alto saxophones. The listeners lie sprawled against the cushions, or pace with detached buoyancy from bare window to bare window. A few words coax out laughs: pot, ball, Eisenhower. Eisenhower? But this must have happened years ago. Kennedy is President now. Not even Kennedy—he is dead. No matter. It has all been preserved on film, 8-millimeter, a little scratchy, a blurred hand-held look, but the music still sounds great and some of the faces are recognizable. It was a historic afternoon compounded of morphine and Benzedrine. Thanks to these tokens we are all permitted to live in the imagination of such a pad.

Johnny Boy and Bad Girl and the Kid walked on, but their destination was not the railroad flats of the larger-than-life poets or the lofts of the alcoholic Zen-influenced painters or the cramped darkrooms of the underground filmmakers, not the obscure boutiques with their Tibetan amulets and incense burners, nor even the clubs (theoretically closed to them by reason of age) from which the political folk singers were beginning to be ousted by the new rock bands singing cryptic songs about meadows full of flowers. (The Kid played bass some and occasionally "sat in" with a group called the Wizards. Bad Girl took guitar lessons and could pick out a few Joan Baez songs and some of the sound track of *A Hard Day's Night*. Johnny Boy stayed up Sundays to hear the new Top 40 listings. Monday morning the first question would be "Did you hear the new Stones song?")

They were not going to those places because, as the children of a prosperous professional class, they had somewhere else to go. Turning north at Fifth, they headed for a splashy apartment building called the Vlaminck (the painter's signature faked on the awning), a dead white facade bellying inward toward a uniformed porter and a false fountain. It was a domain of explosive orange carpeting (synthetic fabric), a garish splotchy canvas said to be "abstract," and a purring elevator lifting them instantly to the penthouse floor. The father was an important surgeon who collected South Asian artifacts. Laotian arhats and an array of Kwan-Yins perched on high shelves, unapproachably valuable. The empty duplex was a paradise. Shag rugs and deep soft sofas made a wonderful playground. (This outward luxury was of course only part of the picture. The absent parents—although it meant precious little to their offspring—also contributed to liberal and worthy causes. Their hidden palace would have felt incomplete had they not, to keep the evil spirits at bay, raised money for hunger and research.) No dust was ever visible even when the sun streamed in across the neighboring pseudo-Gothic spires.

There were many such islands. Word got around about them. The son of the blacklisted physicist was giving a party next weekend. The apartment goes on forever—twelve rooms, fourteen rooms—and he's got it all to himself. The father committed suicide. You know the case—probably innocent, railroaded by Nixon and McCarthy—and the son grew up on psychiatrists and narcotics. All his friends went to some traditionally left-wing high school on the Upper West Side. They take drugs, heroin, that is, with actual needles. They call it "shit." They are said not to be very nice; they appear rather sullen when confronted by teenagers from other schools. Their relatives, the kindly old socialists, don't understand what has happened. They weep, they scream about turning them in to the police. The kid turns up the stereo and shuts the door.

There's another who wears a snazzy wristwatch and expensive perfume, and has wintered in Cairo and Nairobi. Her lawyer father (oh, the unmeasurable power of these fathers!) is close to the Kennedys. But there the rug was Afghan and the table mahogany—and wasn't that a Klee half-visible through the door of the old man's "den"? He came out for five minutes to watch her dancing to "Get Off My Cloud." His youngest son sells nickel bags of marijuana to junior high kids.

Nobody wanted to state the obvious: We are the luckiest teenagers in the history of the world. We have been given cozy and well-protected suites in which to be feverishly condemned, to rip open cigarette packs, soak up night air and stereo music, stroll to the refrigerator to steal the father's imported ale. We thread a path between the piano and the venetian blinds, enjoying a theater consisting of a wide rug bounded by mirroring surfaces, metalwork, earthenware, small delicate glass objects. Pulling from the shelf a book containing really wild Austrian paintings: there are some great things hidden in there if you know where to look. We've inherited some fabulous floor space.

All that's really needed is a place to talk. Talk can go on forever. The new Stones song is about amphetamine. Is about condoms. Is tough. They sing flat, it sounds great. That riff at the end! Barbara thinks she is hip, but she isn't. Hip people do not read fashion magazines, they read the Pocket Poets series. They don't read, they taunt the police and play loud music. Are you afraid, does it sound too dangerous? The Fugs are going to be in Tompkins Square. The words are obscene. The new teacher is a real fascist. He's prissy. We were accused of smoking in the bathroom. Linda is not a virgin. William Burroughs is serious. I'm upset about my self image, about my mother, about feeling ghostlike. Did you hear what I dreamed? We made love in the middle of a burning bus. Sex should be honest and free. Should be independent of race and creed. Her cousin was taken by the doctor and measured. It sounds so disgusting. The scars are from slashing her wrists. The new Stones song is about what Camus meant when he talked about suicide. There is only one truly serious philosophical question and that is suicide. An empty heart is like an empty life. Have you ever felt like that? I feel like that all the time. I feel like that right now. We are going to create a conspiracy of high school students. A secret nation will be created out of all the hip people meeting after school. Smuggle in wine and illicit books, have clandestine meetings in the library. Use certain words and buttons as codes. I could work as a waitress and we could rent a house and live in it together. What fun we'd have! Can you imagine a world invented by us?

Something had changed; there had been a detour. Once it might have been easier to be Archie and Veronica: to shop for mod jackets and "kicky" accessories in pastel shades of blue and pink, to make an official tour of the glassy boutique with its imported bath lotions and after-shaves. An introduction to the art of wine-tasting is scheduled as a pregraduation exercise. Afterward Bad Girl and all the other girls are assembled into a prom line. The gym is awash in tuxedos and glamour. A benign etiquette grants permission to drink spiked punch, permission to wear high-heeled shoes.

It had been a world of carefully laid tracks. The door leads into the hall. The key fits the lock. The clothes go on in a particular sequence and the parts of the body are washed in a particular sequence. You walk out of the designated exit and are paid money; are a circulation manager. It has been made to mesh. It's for this that the girls were to have been saved: to be placed in a proper home, to have a table reserved, to be part of a list of donors. There is a mechanism within which we can lead comfortable and satisfying lives, while at the same time fulfilling obligations. Welcome aboard.

The invisible boundaries (surrounding, for example, the duplex) were not intended to be breached. There was not supposed to be a way in. But the kids come in and gain unapproved access to all the interiors. Scavengers of the precious run careless fingers along the porcelain, smear the inlaid photos of Hindu erotica, and now (unrolling a wad of dirty cellophane) pour a clump of earthy herb across the glass.

Drugs were a dream come true. Not just the dream of Allen Ginsberg, or Charlie Parker, or Aldous Huxley, but the dream of Coleridge and De Quincey and Baudelaire and Rimbaud. The usual adult pleasures—gin, six-packs, Winstons—were harsh and palpable, offering buffets of rough gusto and shrieks of merriment, an occasion to pinch bottoms or roll down staircases. The parents in their party hats roared their presence. The insensitivity! How could any of that compare with the mysterious substances—hashish, opium—imbued with reveries of odalisques and glimmering statuary and silken fabric billowing to the accompaniment of a droning oud?

In an imaginary room in the nineteenth century, poets smoke

from long hookahs and ascend in rapt silence toward the ecstasy that will engender "Kubla Khan" or *The Illuminations*. Now, a century away, Johnny and his friends were trying to find a way back into that room. There are other things to love in life—girls, movies, sunny days at the beach—but they are *outward* things. We want the inside track, the secret world available for only five bucks from a guitarist who hangs out at Reggio's.

Drugs were the fundamental text. If you had not read the book, you couldn't participate in the discussion that followed. A spiritual elite clustered in upstairs bedrooms, spraying air freshener or burning incense as camouflage, settling down to enjoy the dismemberment of language, the modification of short-term memory, the vivid jabs of discontinuity and timelessness. Loss of gravitational pull—a "rush"—made them lean back and surrender to the takeoff of their imaginary rocket. By quaint coincidence a record called *The Ventures in Space* was playing, and appeared to have been playing for a very long time; they had never noticed the pauses between the sounds before.

Thereupon Bad Girl, having all at once understood the function of space and time, burst into explanation: It goes on forever, it cancels itself out, everything corresponds to everything else, the faces that seem to be faces are really just the mirrors answering back from the other side of the stars. "We are inside the galaxy right now. This spot is in outer space as much as any other. Isn't that far out?" There had never existed such a feeling of awe. They looked with new and alienated eyes at their surroundings: certainly the impersonal spigots and draperies, the radiator and upholstery and ungainly furniture had not been designed as a setting for these visions. Someday they would have to design new houses. It was like a birth: "Nobody realizes this except us." By then, having lapsed from high silence into words, it would be time to smoke some more and watch television with the sound turned off, changing channels as rapidly as possible to produce the most comical juxtapositions, while wolfing down Devil Dog after Devil Dog. Eye and ear had never been acuter. On the walk to the subway the city's molecules squirmed delicately. The greens and reds of a Nedick's had the lightweight solidity of a rock formation in Cézanne. This etherealization of grille and neon was presumably what was meant by the phrase "beauty of form."

If Johnny Boy had been able to articulate his attitude toward Bad Girl, he might have said: I wanna contemplate you. Marijuana had a delicious effect on her presence; time slowed down and so it seemed he was sitting next to her even longer than he was. If time could be stopped altogether, then she would never leave. Getting high together was like an interlude of eternity: everything was happening *in here*. Outside was just constant motion, disorienting noise, blurred bodies disappearing around corners.

He remembered one afternoon leaning over a high school desk with her, looking at an illustration in *The Psychedelic Review*. She had brought it to school, hidden, another of the tools or weapons or treasures she liked to surprise people with: "You have to see this!" The illustration was a flowerlike mandalic pattern (but they were not yet acquainted with the word "mandalic") painted by a Navajo Indian under the influence of peyote. They knew what peyote was; they had studied the writings of Aldous Huxley and Robert S. DeRopp, and had pinpointed the relevant passages in every book published by City Lights or Grove Press; they knew that peyote was legal for some Indians because it was part of their religion ("Isn't that wild!"), that it was consumed in the form of foul-tasting buttons, that it frequently induced vomiting prior to its visions. They traded such information like baseball cards.

Much of *The Psychedelic Review* was an impenetrable mass of Latin plant names, chemical formulas, and methodological jargon ("35 persons were resident . . . for the purpose of studying the transpersonative effects of group interaction with the concurrent use of LSD-25"). But in that flower image, at once inviting and alien, they could come to rest. She whispered (class was going to start in a couple of seconds) how nice it would be to take peyote in the southwestern desert, at night, in a cave, on a plain, to spread out a blanket, to paint a picture like that. Imagine the silence and the solitude for hundreds of miles, wouldn't you like to do that someday? *There are people who do. There are places you can go to do things like that.* Johnny Boy could barely shape a reply, caught in the chastely erotic enchantment of hallucinatory pistils and stamens, flowers of vision budding covertly within the classroom. They exchanged conspiratorial winks.

One of the functions of the cabal was to secretly film their own lives. Songs were the sound track of the movie they were making together. Rooms and sidewalks were enlisted into a dramatic geography. Four or five of them converging on a school dance became an exciting cinematic gesture, a fluid balletic dolly shot whose graininess emphasized the "reality" of the image. *Cinéma vérité* had been invented recently. Just imagine if you could film everything that happened. Or make a movie about a party that went on forever, with all the beer and cigarettes and music and people falling down, moaning, confessing to each other at three in the morning. And we will all star in it. You'll play the Burt Lancaster part, you'll be Kim Hunter, you'll be Richard Basehart. I'll be John and you'll be Paul and you'll be—the Beatles' girlfriend, or the girlfriend of the Rolling Stones. The girl the song was written about. Or else you'll be Monica Vitti staring at the camera, passionate and expressionless. But that was in a different movie.

The important thing was to walk with a certain graceful strength, to have style, to display a wicked charm, a roguish insouciance, to hit the high ones every time out, to be indifferent to one's own

magnetism, to be Bogart or Astaire or Errol Flynn in his deca-
dence, falling drunkenly off the yacht in *Too Much, Too Soon*. Or
else one could wear mod collars and be the Kinks. The television
appearance was sketched in memory as a few seconds of jagged
angularity, to be summoned up a thousand times: Did you see
them on "Shindig"? You didn't? And then try, yet again, to
describe that which passes description.

In a blue haze the gang walks into the school dance. They feel
like incandescent shadows. The same Stones song keeps insisting
"an empty heart is like an empty life" and at the end Mick Jagger
or somebody chants in falsetto "I wanna die." In one moment—
the crowd fuzzy in the smoke, the boy and girl smiling ecstatically
at each other in response to the harmonica part—it becomes a
patented memory. As the harmonica part recurs, the smile of
interpenetration recurs, clicking into place like constellations into
their orbits. It will be their "signature tune." Played two hundred
times, the song will yield each time the same chunk of data,
consisting (roughly) of bright eyes, dim party lights, sense of the
two of them constituting a world apart, sense of two bundles of
molecules almost tearing loose, sense of the void.

Apart from all this darkness and smokiness and emptiness, it
was beginning to be a golden age of teen sex. Unfortunately, they
were not told until the last moment. A grandmotherly woman
from the family planning clinic came to school to tell them that
sexuality was uplifting when accompanied by tenderness. Swedish
and Danish schoolchildren, for instance, were now issued, along
with their bus passes and library cards, high-spirited manuals on
contraception and masturbation. *Candy* and *Tropic of Capricorn*
had just become licit; people just slightly older than themselves,
on the other side of high school, were routinely "living together";
and toward the whole topic of "making it" an air of casual but
persistent interest—a sort of intellectual dedication—could now

be openly affected. The era of sexual agony was over. The Pill had come. They had been exempted from the war of the body.

What a dawn it was; and yet it could never quite be the fresh start of which they dreamed. The Western sexual tradition kept getting in their way. They would have liked to write it an open letter: Why did you do this to us? You have blighted the fun house that would have been our bodies. Even Blake and Shelley said so hundreds of years ago. We try to take off our clothes but are unable to take off the idea of them. We encounter thickets of thwartings: "My baby's got me locked up in chains, but they ain't the kind that you can see." Why isn't my girlfriend happy? How can we smash what ten thousand years of language have done to our bodies? How could desire become a burden? I insist on knowing how this was permitted to happen.

The fathers and mothers repeat the law code of the ancestors. Who can we blame but some ancient villain—Vincent Price in *The Pit and the Pendulum* or Charlton Heston in *The Ten Commandments*—for what Dr. Wilhelm Reich (master, it is whispered, of forbidden knowledge) called "the invasion of compulsory sex-morality"? (She showed Johnny the paragraph about the formation of adolescent character armor and they both felt helpless.)

The teenagers, fresh adults, construct a scale model of the outside world. With great ingenuity they mix martinis and make love in a bed by daylight. The angle of the cigarette in the hand accentuates the blinds just like in *Written on the Wind* or *All That Heaven Allows*. It was a very grown-up sort of afternoon. But soon enough they would be mailing their postcard from the material world: "Situation desperate. Please come through soon. Transfiguration urgently requested."

Why so desperate so instantly? Is it because of the shelves, the telephone, the ashtray—these mute totems of a system the kids are on the verge of dominating? They tiptoe around the wiring and feel uncomfortable. It is a world of edges, surfaces, distances between things. At moments it seems as stiff and artificial as the Victor Mature movie they watched last night. In this context the way they feel about their bodies becomes peculiar: the flesh itself is another belt, another pair of pants. Its edge, the fact that it has an edge, confines.

It touches things, the body does, with its hands: but do the things know they are touched? The manmade furniture presents a mien of complete indifference. Impossible to be alone in such a room, where the objects do not even acknowledge one's presence; where, living, one experiences already the nullity of not existing. (I underlined, and showed her, the passage in Kierkegaard where he seems to say something similar. We agreed that he had "really said it." Sartre had said it, too, and Camus; but it was cold comfort.)

I, for instance, move toward you, in the hope of moving toward an aeration of this too solid body. But I must walk on the rug, negotiate a path between sofa and coffee table (why did our parents buy such harsh and heavy furniture?), being careful not to bruise my shin or knock over the glass on the table's edge, and then confront (in the space between our eager minds) such things as buttons and elastic waistbands, in whose awkward interstices the folds of the body itself seem lost. And (this never ends) I must turn the television on, or off. I must change the channel on the radio to get away from the irritating song. I must stack up three LPs of enlivening music, because in silence the room is too utterly hard and bare. The thick drapes are a clutter and even the softest furniture is hard. Let's get out of here!

But the body never ends. The quality of being a thing never ends. Bright lights and cocktails and more cigarettes are imported to deal with the problem. If there are too many things, let's have more things, only make them fun things this time. Spaces are created through an appropriate positioning of cushions, but the spaces are never wide enough. The room is never big enough. So we get more rooms. But there are never enough of them. When you are in the living room you want to be in the bedroom, and when you are in the bedroom you want to be in the living room. When it is night you want it to be day again; when it is early you want it to be late; when you are full you want to be hungry so you can begin again. Some people are never satisfied.

Bad Girl believed in Free Love. The way she said it, it sounded like a crystal palace full of fountains and flower beds. Johnny thought it was the best idea he had ever heard there was to be no envy, no possession, no pain—except that in practice it meant she slept with a lot of guys, and he was denied even the satisfaction of berating her for it. Instead he was obliged to berate himself for lack of sophistication, for clinging to a kind of D. W. Griffith moral drama in which Lillian Gish, the White Flower of the South Seas, was perennially cast on the reefs of lechery and exploitation. A free girl just couldn't go anywhere without being set upon by predators, many of them unassailably stylish and worldly-wise. It was the main problem he had with the idea of freedom.

In the meantime, in his gloom, he listened to songs. He never quite knew whether his emotions gave character to the song, or the song to his emotions. If he had not heard the Zombies sing "Tell Her No," would he have imagined some such miniature music drama anyway—or had the Zombies simply invented a new mode of feeling? After a while it seemed that every song—every *good* song—defined an emotion which did not exist outside that song. No song could ever substitute for another. There was only one "Another Girl" or "Pretty Flamingo" or "Ooo, Baby Baby." Ultimately there could be a list of thousands of isolated emotions, like a seed catalog.

There was a reservoir of feeling that irrigated existence. The parents, desiccated, were mostly cut off from it. They lived, many of them, in old apartments within upended cracker boxes grouped around one another like so many Comstock wagons to shut out the hostile city. The geometric paths and stone fountains within these housing developments must have been intended to make the "towns" and "villages" truer to their absurd names. The formal interconnections—circular hedges, converging halls, lobbies emerging from the shrubbery as if in welcome—symbolized a system of warm relationships, of tribal patterns that unfortunately were no longer even a memory. The tiny groups—father, mother, daughter, son—lived isolated in cramped spaces. They were surrounded by necessary but uncomfortable objects—window screens, refrigerators, ironing boards—under circumstances in which the shutting or opening of a door, the adjusting of a thermostat, the turning of a radio dial were major events.

It was just another box within a box, its windowpanes and doorjambs identical down to the nails and the flaked paint. The stove and the toilet and the doorbell had stations as fixed as any font or nave: it was only a sacred function that they lacked. The offspring who had grown within these cages felt themselves to be the victims of architecture, their lives and minds shaped by hostile furniture. The vestibule oppressed. The bedroom wall was where they did not want there to be a wall. The layout of the rooms embodied decisions made before they got here.

And in the places where empty space would have been, there were instead roped-up bundles of yellowing newspapers, precious ancient magazines, brittle plastic albums of memorabilia—Uncle Jack at Silver Lake, your father at the bank dinner—that could never be moved or thrown away. The inherited heaps were pressed on one another, just as the building was pressed on its identical neighbors, a crowd of rectangular shapes shored up against the invasion of light. They were kept meticulously clean and very little noise ever issued from them. The things preserved within them seemed symptoms of mourning, fragments of a death ritual. The owners superstitiously worshipped objects that made them unable to forget, even for a second, who and where they were.

So the kids slipped out of the choked home, a bottle of chianti hidden under the duffel coat, and went to hide among the stairs. There were twenty flights of them, a metallic landscape apt for discussions of time and suicide. There, fired by wine, Johnny Boy and Bad Girl sprawled against the railing and gestured toward the empty universe around them. The stairwell was in the heart of a spiral. Space extended infinitely above and below, and the bare walls and black metal somehow emphasized the surges of energy that the two of them were burning up as fast as they could feel them coming. Rolling to one side, climbing half a flight for a more emphatic angle, enjoying the coldness of the steps as if that certified their existence, Johnny Boy and Bad Girl felt modern ideas pouring out of them uncontrollably. The world was as negative, deadpan, and hard-edged as a Jean-Luc Godard movie, and they were right in the middle of it.

Strange things were happening all over. Even in the neighboring suburbs the teenagers were getting intense. They drove cars through their fathers' picture windows. The police cordoned off the town and arrested all the rich kids for selling narcotics to ninth graders. A boy and girl—"so sensitive, so intelligent"—joined in a suicide pact to protest the war in Vietnam. Would you do that? Why not—we have to destroy ourselves one way or another, don't we? There is nothing so terrible as ennui. Delirium is a disease of the night. Words float through the city like garbage. The trick is to be two things at once: inside you are tragic (melancholy, self-lacerating, alienated, moody, depressed, death-haunted), outside you are hip (clipped, stylish, tough, offhand, lean, poker-faced). You engage in black humor instead of shrieking or weeping. You are fun to be with. You steal pills and are caught. You watch old Marlene Dietrich movies and are amused. You talk about the end of the world and what will happen afterward. You look cute in a beret. You memorize criminal slang and practice to be the moll of a drug dealer, a waiflike sidekick. You are in search of your destiny; you've found it; it isn't there. Either everything is full of shit or everything is sublimely serious. You draw the childlike purple flower and then you rip it up. You dress in black, become as pale as possible, and utter shocking obscenities. You grit your teeth.

This disjointed seesawing between the flip and the bleak denoted seriousness. The less serious teens could adore Paul McCartney, join in sing-alongs, stay home to watch "I Dream of Jeannie" or "Mission: Impossible"; or, having been forced to sit through the entire Bob Dylan record, say, "I don't understand what he's so hostile about. I mean, what's his problem?" To be countered, naturally, with, "You wouldn't understand."

You wouldn't understand because you haven't been marked with the stigmata of the psychological caseworker: "substance abuse" and "promiscuity" and "personality disorder." You are, perhaps, the blessed one of whom it could be written: "has an outgoing personality, mixes well with others, shows a readiness to take on adult responsibilities." But Bad Girl's malaise was already written down in a number of files: "A. seems to have a complex of problems relating to group interaction. She responds to authority in a hostile manner and encourages a delinquent attitude in others. She is reluctant to participate in group activities, becoming withdrawn or sometimes openly uncooperative. By preference she seeks out antisocial cliques rather than socializing with the class as a whole. She has on several occasions been caught smoking cigarettes on school property, is frequently late to school or absent altogether, and is widely rumored to have been involved in more serious misconduct. Her pallor, nervousness, and apparent fatigue indicate a possible need for medical attention." In earlier days they had called her highly imaginative and creative, with a wonderfully offbeat sense of humor.

One day Bad Girl didn't show up. Word filtered through that she had been spirited off to "an institution." All her bad habits were under official scrutiny now. It was early spring, and in the warm weather people were listening to what seemed like the sweetest music ever made. The Beatles were making serious records with sitars and harpsichords and ambiguous lyrics, and then the rest of the time there were Otis Redding and Martha and the Vandellas and Sir Mack Rice. Even the Beach Boys were releasing inconclusive minor-key songs with just the right shape to qualify as modern; and a French critic had called Procol Harum's "A Whiter Shade of Pale" "the most important musical event since the death of Bach." It was pleasant to live in the middle of a renaissance. The words "youth" and "love" did not sound amiss to the young and loving; it seemed rather as if the world had come to their door. They walked through Central Park talking of Bad Girl, and when they got past Bethesda Fountain they rented a boat and rowed along the leafy shore. They let the boat drift under the bridge and continued to talk of Bad Girl until they ran out of things to say. She was already a legend.

To Johnny—suddenly tightening his grip on the oar—she seemed in danger of becoming just an idea. If he thought about her he might end up going off on some wild flight—"existentialist gang girl, blond mask, death-vigil penitent"—and forget who *she* was, simply because she wasn't there to see every day. In her absence her image became stronger, but who made that image? In class hadn't they read the "Lamia" of Keats, with its gorgeous phantom conjuring up her psychically contrived palace, and then didn't they go to see *Vertigo* (it had just been re-released) where Jimmy

Stewart fell in love with a mirror image and then kept kicking the glass until he bled? He felt her image changing in his mind, and hoped that one day he'd have a chance to discuss it with her.

They had had many serious conversations, and the centerpiece of those conversations was always the word "mind." They talked about minds communicating with each other across great distances, and they talked about Mind as an eternal state that everybody came from and went back to and always made part of. Yet now she was gone, and there was no way to reach that mind! He concentrated and repeated her name but nothing happened.

It seemed they ought to be able to mount an assault on the hospital and carry her off, like Robin Hood and his merry men. They would strike like lightning and then vanish into the forest where they would establish a socialist democracy containing free drugs, suckling pigs roasting on spits, and poets and musicians improvising jazz ballads in glades. She was, after all, one of their own. But they were teens, powerless against the conspiracy of parents and psychiatrists and policemen.

In the interim there were ways to keep amused. The world was full of things that summer. You might, if you were fortunate, go to Europe or Montauk so that your friends could joke and call you "jet set." Or you could stay in town to catch the Four Tops (their new single sounded like Bob Dylan—"if you can imagine Dylan as Motown!"—and was a work of genius) at the Basin Street East, go see *Torn Curtain* opening day (the killing scene was something else), or stay up drinking Budweiser and watching *The Tijuana Story* or *Werewolf in a Girl's Dormitory* on "The Late, Late Show." He lifted his beer can, thinking, "If I could just stop thinking about her," and before long he got his wish. The normal pleasures of a human being were all right, as it turned out—why make war on the context that made possible movies, cocktails, seafood restaurants? It was not so bad to grow up possessing a briefcase, an elegant car, a sheaf of tickets to the great cities. Things were getting livelier every day in the big world. The stock market went through the roof and the businessmen started wearing paisley ties. The fashion business was doing great, the television business was doing great, the music business was in delirium. The middle class was having more fun than it had ever thought possible. There was a war, yes, and murderous riots, but inside the secure zone the mood was as giddy as an episode of "Laugh-In," as splashy as an Op Art cocktail dress designed by Yves Saint Laurent.

One afternoon, amid the luxuriant heat of Park Avenue, surrounded by bright clothes and gleaming cameras, Johnny was struck by a sudden memory of Bad Girl's face, ghostly white after one of her bad nights. She was trying to complete a statement about the nature of reality, but its point kept eluding her. Her syntax disintegrated, became circular; and all the while she clutched her new amulet, a faceted plastic pendant that gave off little kaleidoscopic flashes. Where had all the fun gone? Her face seemed part of a seductively painful dream it was time to wake from.

ACID
REVOLUTION

Early in July two odd girls in shapeless black dresses sat in the living room listening to the new Beatles album. In those days a new Beatles album was an event. Friends gathered to share the freshness of the never-to-be-recaptured first hearing. The girls, however, seemed surprisingly indifferent, as if they had better things to think about. Only when the last song came on did they show signs of interest, leaning forward to catch the lyrics, hatching little smiles of satisfaction, until one of them remarked, "Do you hear what he's singing? That's exactly what Dr. Leary teaches." Afterward they asked that the song be repeated. (Of course, it was precisely the song that everyone else would have preferred to skip: "Must we sit through that droning again?")

It was still, at that moment, permissible to ask: "Who is Dr. Leary?" The answer was somewhat circuitous. The girls were living, it appeared, in an enormous house in upstate New York. It was a paradise, like nothing you could imagine. They spent their time—studying? experimenting? meditating? It was difficult to know the right word to use with strangers. "Have you read *The Tibetan Book of the Dead*? We are learning to understand death and rebirth. Most people are stuck in one bardo or another. Dr. Leary teaches us how to go through all that, you know, distinguish reality from illusion, and see the white light." Her face certainly was white, a pasty whiteness perhaps associated with the macrobiotic diet she had been discussing a moment earlier. There was evidently a close connection between mucus formation and the stubborn persistence of ego-oriented thought patterns. Her words didn't reveal much, but they lingered in the mind the way unfamiliar jargon always does. Later you'd say to a friend, "Were you aware that 'Tomorrow Never Knows' has something to do with a sort of religious cult?" It was unusual to meet religious people of any kind.

In late August people streamed back into Manhattan. Those returning from London and Paris spoke of hair and music, cinémathèques and galleries, splendid wine-drenched sunsets along the Quai Voltaire. They spoke most enthusiastically of the past, and of the wonderful things emerging from it: the art nouveau masterpieces excavated in the basements of museums, the impossibly beautiful *films noirs* gazed at in tiny Parisian movie theaters. A bottomless cache of precious artifacts had been secreted a few decades back, all for our delectation in this present age of pleasure: surrealist French serials, old comic strips, the piano music of Satie and the ballads of Billie Holiday, fashion magazines of the thirties, room after room filled with gorgeously kitschy figurines of languid nymphs fashioned out of industrial plastic. The travelers had come back to embellish New York with their treasures.

But what of the one who had gone, somewhere in May or June, out to California? It was already September and still no word from the Coast. Then in October a phone call: "I can't talk because there's so much going on, you wouldn't understand. A new age is beginning. I know you'll think I'm crazy, but there are people out here who are starting a new civilization. I'm talking about sensitive intellectuals, poets, people like you. It's the biggest revolution in the history of the world. Remember I told you first! It's a new way of living. I'll tell you all about it at Christmas. It's going to be wonderful!" And in parting: "None of it makes any sense at all unless you take acid. There is literally no other way to grasp it."

Rivulets of hearsay began to fill in the blanks of what had been designated a new spirit. The new slang filtered through. It was no longer about cynicism. People were trying to be as unsarcastic as possible. The days of existential angst were played out. (But you knew that already, didn't you? All that came to an end as soon as *Time* started talking about the Theater of the Absurd.) The new phase in history had begun, rolling out of San Francisco like the philosophical equivalent of the frug.

What would it be like to feel happy? It was as if the question had never been asked before. A few years earlier the traces of actual merriment surfacing in *A Hard Day's Night* had successfully defused whole categories of intellectual doubt. Yet the bubbliness of Pop and Op and Julie Christie was admittedly a flat display. The luminous idols were enamored of their own elegant vacancy and had a capacity (otherwise known as "style") for letting us share fleetingly in that love: the entertainer's smile expressed his pleasure in anticipating our pleasure in seeing that smile. But what if the Beatles had real bodies, and were not simply two-dimensional speeded-up clips of celluloid or carefully blurred studio snapshots? Soon even the Beatles would be publicly asking that question, affirming that they too had reached the limits of a world consisting of the gazers and the gazed-at. In a more evolved situation (the logic ran) the star would be an actual person capable of responding to you. The Beatles had already moved in this direction by seeming to act as spokesmen for their listeners, fellow participants in a common wave of activist tenderness. Perhaps, having absorbed such unprecedented bombardments of love from their audience, they had been obliged—positively *forced*, by some arcane electromagnetic process—to channel that love into equally unheard-of forms. By this theory the Beatles became conduits for the collective energy of their fans, which same energy having traveled through the Beatles came out the other side as music: music returning to the fans who sent it out, like a lost body. A community was implicit, however random or fragmented.

But to realize such a community would mean going through or beyond the sender/receiver deadlock. The implements of the age of communication, records and movies and television, simply weren't communicating enough. There had to be more than a screen, otherwise even the most intimate experiences felt weirdly inauthentic. The "media" (the name was still fresh) promised the world and then everyone felt disappointed. As if to minister to that letdown came Dr. Leary's newest thoughts, contained in a little pamphlet entitled *Start Your Own Religion*. It began as if from far away, a voice deep in paradise intoning glutinous sentences redolent of strange ecstasies: "That intermediate manifestation of the Divine Process which we call the DNA Code has spent the last two billion years making this planet a Garden of Eden." But how to get back there? Leary's formula became the standard—if usually misquoted—text for explicating the aims of "the LSD cult" (as it was then known): "DROP-OUT—detach yourself from the external social drama which is as dehydrated and ersatz as TV. TURN-ON—find a sacrament which returns you to the Temple of God, your own body. Go out of your mind. Get high. TUNE-IN—be reborn. Drop-back-in to express it. Start a new sequence of behavior that reflects your vision."

Leary was playing with fairly sophisticated marketing techniques: the clipped "Go out of your mind. Get high" was superb. But he fell short of Madison Avenue ideals by succumbing to social science lingo ("external social drama," "sequence of behavior") and, worse, the totality-of-cosmic-unity link-it-all-up style of mannered hyphenation represented by "drop-back-in." (In time, the weblike interstices of acid prose would so clot with internal connections that sentences could barely find it in themselves to end.) Excising the hyphens and the wordy commentary, the phrase boiled down to "Drop Out, Turn On, Tune In": almost right, except it didn't quite fall trippingly on the tongue. Turn it around— never mind the violation of Leary's logical progression, such as it is—and it became "Tune In, Turn On, Drop Out," a far more appropriate slogan for printing on buttons or on the kind of placards invariably waved by acid heads on TV programs and in comic books.

Lest anyone misconstrue, Leary was careful to add: "Don't vote. Avoid all politics. Do not waste conscious thinking on TV-studio games. Political choices are meaningless. . . . No rebellion— please!" He envisaged considerably more archaic political forms: "A group liberation cult is required. You must form that most ancient and sacred of human structures—a clan. A clan or cult is a small group of human beings organized around a religious goal. . . . You must start your own religion. You are GOD—but only you can discern and nurture your divinity. . . . Center on your clan and the natural order will prevail."

Such declarations, with their unabashed tribal yearnings sounding curiously like the *Völkischer* outpourings of some Hitlerian bard, contrasted with the sceptical leftish context in which they often appeared. *The East Village Other*, for instance, had started out in October 1965 as a raunchy, playful diary of Lower East Side artistic and political activity in the era of happenings, underground movies, New York poets, Ban the Bomb, Fair Play for

Cuba, and Ed Sanders' Peace Eye Bookstore. But by mid-'66 the harmless eccentricities of old-line Bohemians and the pious certitudes of *vieux jeu* Marxists were no longer enough: a portentous, messianic strain began to dominate, its focal point none but Dr. Leary (by now under federal arrest on the flimsiest of drug raps), "the guru of hundreds of thousands of youthful spirits who thank him very much for exploring what might prove to be the way to end war." Or, as more categorically enunciated by Arthur Klebs, Chief Boo-Hoo of the Neo-American Church: "The discovery of LSD may be taken as the intervention of God in human history.

I see no moral difference whatever between putting our religious leader, Timothy Leary, in prison for thirty years and the incarceration of a Rabbi in a concentration camp by the Gestapo of Nazi Germany. Perhaps Hitler was less hypocritical." And finally there was Allen Ginsberg, smiling a bit uncertainly as he posed (March 1967) in the entrance gate of Auschwitz, to proclaim: "I will make a first proposal . . . that everybody who hears my voice, directly or indirectly, try the chemical LSD at least once, every man woman and child in good health over the age of 14—that, if necessary, we have a mass emotional breakdown in these States once and for all."

So the kids drank the potion. One or two or three at a time, they made contact. They stumbled toward a shining presence that so far consisted mostly of words: "You have to . . . It's the most important . . . the best . . . the most beautiful thing that ever happened to me." Or most horrible. But by now they were aware that "every 'bad trip' is caused by the failure to 'tune in' " (Leary) and that any risks were worth it because (again Leary) "you are not a naughty boy getting high for kicks. You are a spiritual voyager furthering the most ancient, noble quest of man."

They were to be heroes, had already become heroes by the simple act of swallowing the little capsule or licking the dot on the piece of paper. They sat cross-legged on couch or rug preparing to plunge into the unknown, just like Flash Gordon or Siegfried or the troglodyte hero of *One Million B.C.*, and like them anticipating monsters: monsters all the more menacing for being undefined, featureless, not quite real, yet capable of rending you apart. "Monsters from the Id!" cried Dr. Morbius in *Forbidden Planet* upon realizing the psychic nature of the spooky special effect that had already devoured much of the cast. These psychedelic dragons would be no less destructive: they must be defeated, like the Jabberwock in the tulgey wood. ("These are just bardo apparitions. Look through them and they become insubstantial.") It seemed they lurked in forested regions of the mind, in thick undergrowth. Such worn-out images all at once appeared brutally meticulous: the map of the mind was beginning to resemble the geography of a Grimm fairy tale, with lots of dark woods and cozy cottages and subterranean streams, towers in which maidens were sequestered, and holes in the floor through which ugly dwarfs stamped themselves in inarticulate rage. Through it all an understanding voice—an experienced friend serving as your "guide"—soothed you: all you have to do is kill the dragon and then you marry the princess and have a happy ending. The ordeal does end eventually. "It's all just your mind anyway"—as if that were reassuring.

Everybody knows the ancient tales. You come to them at bottom when everything else has drained away. They are sequences of magical events, initiated by a single sign: the ritual dropping of the handkerchief, the plow breaking into the soil. It comes to pass—in an atmosphere positively biblical. After centuries of waiting, it all starts happening just like they said it would. This is not the first time: it's happening *again*, the way it did in your former life, remember? Once you believed you were going to be a travel agent or a professor of Middle European studies. But on reaching the predetermined age (this happens in science fiction novels all the time, perhaps they are true) you find that you have been elected to save the world: "My son, I never told you this before, but . . ." Various ceremonies follow: the taking of a new name, the tempering of the sword, the donning of symbolic regalia. At this point you are formally introduced to the other knights of the Round Table. (Van Morrison would sing: "You can't stop us, on the road we're free . . . Knights in armor bent on chivalry.")

But you don't get the regalia until you are out of the woods. There are things to be done first. Or only one thing, really, and of course it is not a "thing": you must meet the white light. The white what? It's like nothing or nobody, at the end of everything. It contains the shape of everything, but nothing fills it. It isn't *made* of anything. There's no way to describe it: or rather, *you* don't describe *it*, *it* describes *you* if so inclined. Properly speaking, it does not exist; but in that sense nothing else does either. Maybe that was what Heidegger meant by "ground of being," or the Zen Buddhists when they refer to "a kick in the eye." I still don't quite understand. Nobody can make you understand. You have to see it: wedged between two microseconds you see the disappearance of the universe, and it's as if you were moving toward your own origin. That moment of anticipation is it! By the time you realize it, it's already gone. An instant too late you find your glimpse has been abruptly terminated. You're going back through the revolving door, expelled right back where you don't want to go. Reincarnated—again!

Various efforts were made to codify this experience. Leary came out with a jazzed-up version of *The Tibetan Book of the Dead* called *The Psychedelic Experience*, in which the peaceful and wrathful deities of the original *Bardo Thödol* were psychologized, domesticated, transmuted into the ordinary by-products of brain chemistry at work. "It's all in your head." But where—the darker question loomed after reading the full-fledged Tibetan-style Evans-Wentz edition, with its notes and glossaries and cautiously glowing foreword by Carl Jung—where is your head? In what context does it persist? Because if one thing was clear, it was that the Tibetans were not even remotely kidding about the reincarnation business. It was chilling—in the century of airlines and switchboards and Holiday Inns—to wonder even for a second what lay beyond the spatiotemporal fabric we call home. You look around the room and see tables and chairs: they are solid, they are *there*. Such solidity ought to be comforting but isn't. You think about the table still being around after you aren't, and wonder whether you'll remember at the time. In a way you would like to live forever, but in other ways maybe not. What if our whole universe is just a seam, a sleeve lining, within a web inconceivable to us? The chairs and tables wavered for an instant.

The theologians of LSD approached these questions not as playful speculation but as the most solemn of duties. That the white light really existed was a profoundly serious matter. It was your rendezvous in inner space, a split-second opportunity to dump all the ego attachments and vain cravings that were making your life miserable; and if you missed it you were back on the wheel until the next round. Everything in life had to be a preparation for that moment. (There was also, as some amateur explorers would find, such a thing as overrehearsing.)

Despite all the publicity surrounding LSD, the white light with its karmic accoutrements never assumed as much importance for journalists as it did for acid heads. It was too hard to get a handle on something about which absolutely nothing could be said. Finally there was nothing to say but: See for yourself. The "LSD cult" could of necessity have only one doctrine: Take LSD. No paraphrase, whether by Alan Watts or Aldous Huxley or Richard Alpert, amounted to more than a nudge in the right direction. The ancient sages had gone as far as possible toward verbalizing these things, but their words were difficult to mold into press releases. There was nothing you could *do* with Huang Po's teaching that "our original Buddha-nature is, in highest truth, devoid of any atom of objectivity," that "it is void, omnipresent, silent, pure; it is glorious and mysterious peaceful joy—and that is all," or with the central maxim of Padma-Sambhava's *Book of the Great Liberation*: "In its true state, mind is naked, immaculate; not made of anything, being of the Voidness; clear, vacuous, without duality, transparent; timeless, uncompounded, unimpeded, colorless; not realizable as a separate thing, but as the unity of all things, yet not composed of them; of one taste, and transcendent over differentiation." It didn't add up to hard copy. A thousand delicately paralleled words worked overtime to deny the validity of words, while someone nodded enthusiastically on the sidelines: "But yes, that is the whole point, the essence of it. *Intrinsically* nothing can be said; if something could be said, then the phenomenon would not be such as it is and we would not even be sitting here. Can you dig it, man?" On the cover of the book, an eye radiating waves of flame rose out of a lotus: Artist's Conception.

Yet if the acid experience theoretically demanded silence in tribute to its inexpressible nature, few could resist verbalizing it. In fact, the pages of *The San Francisco Oracle* and *Crawdaddy* and *Avatar* and *Innerspace* were stuffed with words running on and on, running together, repeating themselves, sentences stretching themselves out of shape in an effort to pin down the elusive and palpitating crux. An inferior but not untypical example can be found in these lines from "The Psychedelic World," a poem by Bernard Roseman included in the anthology *LSD: The Age of Mind*:

> Little droplets of molten silver
> drop from the heavens.

A blending of sound interwinds
and merges to become pure light.
    Each object exists
               in infinite perfection. A sharp,
                     knife-like distinction
   seems to separate each spectacle. Perfect
cogs spinning
   in opposite directions
      with no other purpose than being.

Strictly this has nothing to do with anything, but a rapidly adopted literary convention established that the use of phrases such as "droplets of molten silver," imprecise abstractions such as "pure," "perfection," and "perfect," and neologisms such as "interwinds" somehow corresponded to taking acid—or stood in as a token for having done so. It was not always easy to say whether my "droplets of molten silver" much resembled your "droplets of molten silver." Interestingly, although LSD was originally touted as a voyage to the heart of your emotional or spiritual problems, the "head literature" tended to focus, like Roseman's poem, on distortions of sound and color and perspective, conjuring up a world of glacial abstraction in which "perfect cogs" have "no other purpose than being." The promised higher reality has become another screen, the ultimate screen because it is taken as a transcendent vision. Hence a traditionally-minded guru like Meher Baba withheld his seal of approval from hallucinogens: "Indulgence in psychedelic drugs is harmful spiritually, mentally, and physically. All so-called spiritual experiences generated by taking 'mind-changing' drugs are superficial and they add enormously to one's addiction to the deceptions of illusion while giving a false glimpse of reality."

For the moment, however, the issue was decided. It was 1967, after all, and it would never come again: LSD rolled through

America like Dior perfume permeating the smoke at a party. As Joel Meltz wrote that summer in *The East Village Other*, "Can a person be human without LSD? Or, let's say, without the psychedelic experience? The answer, as far as the writer of this article can see, is a highly qualified, cautiously rendered, but emphatic, definitely NOT."

THE MYTH OF
THE BIRTH OF
THE HIPPIE

It happened in the season of mayflies.

There are crossroads in the world. This is the first day of the rest of your life. It is the beginning of spring. The stone is rolled away from the tomb. The path by the park bifurcates. At this moment—the buds half-opened, the vegetation swelling in the pavement cracks—the pedestrian caught in a moment of indecision has two choices. He can keep walking in linear fashion toward the plaza with its inorganic rectangles and blanket of exhaust fumes, where he will stand on line for a job in the political system. With sufficient credits he will be exempted from combat duty in the empire's outer zones. Ultimately he will be permitted to occupy a property in which rooms, trees, and lawn acreage have been allotted pro rata: so many credits, so many cubic feet of living space. Not for a moment, once he gets caught in that treadmill, will he know quiet again. Not for one morning will he be permitted to wander off by himself.

Or else—at the outset, while he still has the chance—he can fork off into the serpentine path winding toward the meadow in which structure has been abolished. This stretch of open space, a space the empire would like to quantify out of existence, survives by virtue of rebellion: we will not *have* any numerals. Inchoate globs of shape and color will be the origin of a new language. It starts here. This is no longer a park: this is an unattached patch of ground at liberty in the universe. Once roped off under the slave name "park," now seized and opened up for its rightful purposes: a first small but crucial assault on the system of bound- aries of which "city" and "nation" are larger components.

The indecisive pedestrian stands at the periphery of the heat and dust and incense. Bongo music has drawn him this far. He already wears the establishment uniform of tie, jacket, brown leather shoes. Worry lines crease his myopic young face. He asks what is going on and is told it is a be-in. He then asks, "What do you do at a be-in?" and is told, "You just *be*, is it always necessary to *do? You just be!*" He is left scratching his head, momentarily distracted from the cares of the working day, think- ing half-ruefully that maybe these people are on to something.

Or he is handed a flower or a bead or a brightly colored knick- knack of some description and on asking how much it costs is told—by a young woman in a soft frayed dress of Indian cotton— "It doesn't cost anything, it's *free*," heavy stress on "free," the stress further reinforced by imploring smile (where did she learn to smile like that?) and penetrating gaze. Or so the legend has it.

If there was nothing to do, then there was likewise nothing to say about it afterward. One might calculate the ratio of tiny gold finger cymbals to painted faces, of bandannas to beards, beards to robes, robes to bare-chested bongo players. It was an exercise in collective feeling that worked beautifully for about eight hours, an intuitive slow-motion Busby Berkeley sequence in which everyone had the opportunity to be a single unthinking petal of the flower. For several months there had been much talk about a universal mind dispersed in individual minds. This was its chance to get together with itself. "Someone said to me, 'We are all one,' and I experienced *déjà vu*."

In the crowd there were a hundred barely perceptible agents. They handed out magenta leaflets or wallet-size photographs of spiritual healers. They peddled everything from nudism to witchcraft; they asserted that in the hidden Gnostic Gospels Jesus preached a regime of vegetarianism and enemas; they extolled various yogis, well established or just coming up; they talked about how sexual freedom could be fused with an anarchosyndicalist economic program. They distributed invitations to their social center on Avenue C. For dozens of budding cults that had practiced through the winter months, it was like a giant audition. Here was their public, primed as it would ever be for the new-minted oracles and exhortations. READ ME! the mimeographed sheets called out, with their misplaced capitals, their clottings of semicolons and ellipses and exclamation marks, their word fusions and compulsive puns. The air of amorphous raggedness befitted either cosmic messages or psychotic effusions.

The central fact about the be-in was that it went on and on. You could swim in it. You could bury yourself in it. A deeply pleasurable boredom emanated from its fluidities and pulsations. Nothing was ever going to happen: just more of the same buzzing around the rock, the swaying of the crowd mesmerized by its own swaying, the monotonous shrieks of kazoos and penny whistles.

It made a picture—unframed, uncentered—whose beauty lay in its vagueness. Nothing was shown in detail: all was smudge and smoke blur and glare. The colors cascaded with pendulumlike regularity. In fact it was better not to see the details of the crowd. It was better not to see what really was going on in the shadows at the field's fringe, or to hear what the bearded balding man was muttering beneath his hypnotic eye contact. At that point the crowd might disintegrate into individuals and thus endanger the pattern it made. It might become less of an art nouveau scroll painting and more of a real-life melodrama of a type not yet conceivable.

It was better that they all remain a visual effect, a cunningly interlaced series of three-dimensional Technicolor icons. The rainbow shirts contrast effectively with the verdant lawn. The beautiful young people dance on the meadow in springtime. The pond nymph is radiant in the beflowered heat. A man sits on a rock and exhibits tranquillity. Another man leaps in the air and exhibits exuberance. Man and woman and child sit naked on the grass to illustrate the familial tenderness of the new age. A goateed man, his hair in pigtails: the shaman. And so on: the juggler, the magician, the extravagant pirate, the spontaneous light-footed maiden symbolizing life energy. You get lost in the thick of it. A bell tinkles. The clouds part. You are utterly absorbed in the conscious tableaux mounted by a generation of displayers: "This is what a free human would look like." "This is the way an ecstatic person might move."

Somewhere within or among or behind all this was knowledge. Where had it come from, and by whose authority was it thus invested? None could answer; least of all those who really knew (by their calm smiles you shall know them), for they were more aware than any of the indefinable nature of the spiritual hierarchies. All this had sprung from an ancient book, from a wordless teaching transmitted from master to master, from a *vibration* as elusive as it was all-penetrating. The people on the lawn all feel it—have done so these last several moments—and you *know* that. Is this perhaps what they used to mean by "revelation"? That would explain a number of things.

Can we put it down on paper, make a list of it? That way we might cut through the moods of distraction, of wavering, of lost focus that beset us all at times. It's hard to hold fast to clear perception. So let's try as best we can to rough out *The Hippie Code*:

1. We are all one.
2. Don't resist the tidal pull.
3. Don't cling to the material: coins, bills, maps, articles of furniture. Door keys. Names.
4. To look at a clock is a life-destroying act.
5. You are afraid of the truth.
6. Time has stopped.
7. I never realized what space was before.
8. It started in Tibet.
9. It started in the depths of the ocean.
10. It started in another galaxy. On another plane of being.
11. It's starting right now.
12. You are already familiar with its moves.
13. We're not going to arrive anywhere. There is no place to reach. This perpetual transit is our home.
14. We are always wide open and in the middle of space. Nowhere to hide.
15. You must not attempt to hide.

Tear up the paper. It wasn't because we wanted laws that we embarked! It's too soon for that kind of thing. Somebody said this is just a foretaste of what the next two thousand years are going to be like. Let's take it slowly, give it a chance to develop. Please don't try to define anything in words: that always kills the fun. Let's enjoy it while it lasts. They already felt the spring slipping away. The blossoms were scattered. The fragile lights and bubbles were increasingly hard to find. They looked all over one another's faces. They began to have conversations, to try and decide what exactly they had seen.

It was the briefest of seasons. They lacked the training to sustain paradise. Your friend became a different being before your eyes, like an ancient tortoise craning its head out of its mossy shell, and you didn't know whether to worship or embrace that being, or even what name to call it. It had been like a guided tour of a theater. They felt privileged to see the wings and flats, the trapdoors and invisible wires, so they might nod in wonder and say, "Aha, that's how the illusion is managed." The trivial room was peeled away to reveal the room within the room, the astral room corresponding to their astral bodies. Belly laughs of terrifying intensity thundered out of them. She said "weeks and weeks" and it was unbearably amusing. How could there be "weeks" of anything, and for that matter what was a "week"? There are no weeks in eternity.

"We have to sit down right now and start everything over again." Ideas streamed out too fast to count. There was so little time and so much to do. First we'll work on language. Too abstract. First we'll work on the family. On the body. On the way we sit. Learn how to smile without thinking, "I am smiling." If we just stop trying to control ourselves, who knows what wonderful stuff will well up.

Our lives henceforth will be very different. My future paintings will depict masklike flower faces writhing and intertwining within an ocher desert. The sunlight in the loft window offers a premonition of what you will see looking down from the mountain studio. By then these transitional forms—disused warehouses converted to living areas, hollowed-out storefronts—will have given way to the mature groves of a rural and philosophical world state. We cluster around the still-smoking pipe (as if in anticipation of the glistening boughs under which we will one day sit) and cast our thoughts toward that epoch without jealousy or money of which we have caught the first faint glimpses.

"It's quite a feeling." They knew what he meant. It was The Feeling: the sovereign spirit. They were inside it; were, so to speak, its atoms. Just as an atom was free, presumably, to bounce out a random path among the other atoms—little suspecting that its randomness was indistinguishable from the most rigorous scientific necessity—likewise B. was free to paint the wall blue, L. to pluck tentatively at a mandolin, and J. to gaze until cross-eyed at the rusty paint flakes heaped at the foot of the radiator. T., in her black spangled dress from Limbo, spent the afternoon stringing colored beads, while the fourth side of *Blonde on Blonde* played again and again. The sweet odor of hashish was a paste binding the various pieces of the world together. The dark Siamese—his name was Hash—looked at the humans through sternly sensual eyes, sensing the awe he inspired in them. Try as they might to change their consciousness, they could never attain his level: he was an emissary of the world they aspired to create.

To find an uncluttered setting for the mind was difficult. The neighboring buildings seethed with rape and murder. The radio crackled out war noise and riot bulletins. Even within their little group, people broke down and accused and wept over sex and family and cash. Mistrust patrolled the eyehole. The police were in the park. A crude handbill filtered in from the street: "Warning. The Mafia is taking over the drug trade. They are diluting the pure herbs and chemicals. The love people are being killed. Brothers and sisters, we must not allow this to happen."

They allowed it to happen. Late reports from the Coast spoke of hippie drug dealers mutilated by the Mob, vice rings commandeering the loving vibes of Haight-Ashbury, veteran acid heads strung out on smack on Telegraph Avenue. The underground papers were getting progressively stranger, more abrasive. One of the editors even said he was God, and was believed. Then word leaked out that LSD had been linked to chromosome damage. (The article in the *Other* began: "Don't read this if you are tripping at this moment, but . . .") And it wasn't even July yet.

Don't think that way. It's just the extraordinarily negative energy around us, the clogged air of the metropolis. It's a reception problem. To clear our heads we have to get out of the maze, find the land, locate the real people, the ones who made it out of the trap.

They are out there somewhere. *Not* in the filthy city whose sole function is to annul the perception of space (space, that is, as defined in the *Chandogya Upanishad*: "We should consider that in the inner world Brahman is consciousness; and we should consider that in the outer world Brahman is space"). *Not* in front of the TV set whose swirl of dots offers a permanent state of not-seeing. *Not* in the apartment cubicle that reinforces the imprisonment of being, the apartment where the lone ego paces its anxious limits and nurtures morbid yearnings for commodities. *Not* walking with extinguished consciousness in the regimented streets, *not* shooting up speed to achieve a delirious mechanization of the whole ego apparatus, *not* feeding on the pornography of glossy fashion ads or on the seductive shadows receding to the far end of the bar.

The poets knew the horror of the cities long ago. Rimbaud: "Monstrous city, night without end!" Georg Trakl: "Oh you dying cities!" And there is no longer any excuse for letting yourself lose your spirit in that waste of metal and stone. The day is over when Baudelaire could write poems about boulevards and smoke, when novelists could drink wine in cafés, when the fur around a woman's shoulder as she stepped from a taxi could be an object for profound contemplation: that myth of urban "life" is no longer permissible.

It was based on insensitivity, on a deluded concept of mind and body that has been cleared away—and how!—by several million micrograms of the new chemistry. And we do not want, anymore, the sick light of these electric bulbs. The tall buildings are obstacles that shut off the sky. The pavement's function is to suppress vegetation. This place is a poison factory. "The city is a zoo for people," as Chicken Hirsch, the drummer for Country Joe and the Fish, put it. "It's a cement zoo for the crazy. It's the same thing as when you take monkeys out of the jungle and put them in cages. They sit there and masturbate. The cities are places where people sit and masturbate." Only Timothy Leary, writing early in '67, offered some hope: "Be prepared for a complete change of American urban technology. Grass will grow in Times Square within ten years. The great soil-murdering lethal sky-scrapers will come down."

But in the meantime there is no space at all. None. There are sections and partitions whose sole purpose is to maim perception. The city is perfect anti-space, constructed entirely of boundaries. The eyes ache from the acrid fumes and the body unconsciously conforms its movements to the rectangular streets and buildings, as if a human being were a wall or a cement slab. The thoughts echo endlessly the hook phrases of jukebox and radio spot and newspaper headline. It takes a big kick—bourbon or amphetamine or violence—to make some space in that flatness. There is nothing here except human beings, and that is a Sahara too awful to imagine. We survive in it by imagining other places. Those oases of the urban spirit, those reveries, what were they but faint in-tuitions of the life of the happy hippies out there somewhere? Their remote presence was as sure as intelligent life on other worlds.

Let's go into the wilderness. On the acid trip the house plants were a miniature replica of that wilderness. They were green gods pulsing in their boxes, as if struggling to poke their way beyond the carpeting and the dusty metal and the general *thingy* quality of the apartment. You had never really paid attention to the shoots before. All of a sudden one of them was talking to you: "Don't worry, we're your friends. You're not crazy. It's just that—this gets a little technical—your mind bumped into some crazy external objects—you were too young to remember—and then it created structures to cope with them and finally it got hard to see past them—the mental structures, that is, not the external objects: although by this time, through a mimetic process, mental structures and external objects were nearly indistinguishable." The stem undulated to indicate an unprecedented verb form. "We, however, understand you perfectly and there is no barrier between us. We'll never give you a hard time." Just then the pussycat— hitherto snarling and evasive—rolled on her back and splayed her hind legs in a posture of trustful abandonment, responding in friendly growls to the altered breathing of the human she shared the room with.

The cat knows! The plant knows! The soil breathes and swells up to answer the foot that presses it! The eyes of the animals are full of knowledge! The flower in the moment of blooming actually experiences ecstasy! The planet itself is a sentient companion! Everything that lives is taking in everything and communicating its response *back* to everything, without stopping, constantly! While the poor dead television just sits there, a hunk of matter alien to the party going on in the universe.

The walls of the urban enclosure open. The dying trees beckon away. The city shrugs, impatient to have done with its own artificiality. Like Faust you slip out the attic window and glide over the roofs. There is so much to be overflown: the warehouse district, the harbor, the gas works by the shore, the three-mile mall, the toy towns of box houses with their little fenced parks, the vast yards of slag and cinder blocks and rusting boxcars. You have to keep going until the land becomes nonhuman.

In the innards of the mountains a sacred lake waits. Choral wolves punctuate the timberline. A solitary stone plummets into the red gorge. The moon rocks in the canyon. The far key hooks back toward the bay. Pine fringe laps at the wind. The forest thickens. It slopes down to the water outlet. The shattered ridge coalesces with its moss. The serpent wriggles across the multi-colored sand. A shelf weathers in the slow foam. There are all these different places out there.

We look at the woods and think unavoidably of a single universal mind gone utterly into form. The sound of the stream continuously running neutralizes the insidious flow of human thoughts. Here is our point of origin. Once you hook into that rhythm there's no need to think again. The movements of stars, migratory patterns, planting cycles, the chirping of insects in their seasons will collaborate to guide you. Nature talks, you listen. Your nerve ends readjust. The staccato of the city language fades. There is no longer any way to be "indoors," no way to be cut off from the soil and the rotting leaves and the bugs. If you don't belong here you don't belong anywhere.

So you just sit out under the starlight with your (select one) (jug of moonshine) (pipe of hashish) (tab of psilocybin), your buttocks comfortable on the (smooth stone) (dried reeds) (soft turf), taking in the cosmic music of the (birds) (wind) (surf), letting your unfocused eye drift at random over the (ocean) (valley) (sky).

That, simply, is bliss.

IVY LEAGUE
BOYS

The college boys sat under the trees trading comic books, an *Iron Man* for a *Daredevil*, gazing speechless at two-page spreads or debating the implications of a new plot development. They felt humility and profound gratitude for Stan Lee's protean imaginative powers, which had transformed Marvel Comics into a crucial cultural enterprise. It was, as one of them remarked, like watching *The Odyssey* being written. They could only hope to be worthy of such a privilege.

Once comic books had consisted of minimalist kiddy fare like *Batman* (the TV version of which had nearly killed off both Pop *and* camp with its heavy-handedness) or *Archie* (useful only as a repository of sexual stereotypes). Marvel was a new birth, a reinvention of narrative that even questioned the idea of art object as discrete entity. In Stan Lee's model of a fluxing and multileveled universe, the nearest event—Peter Parker boarding the crosstown bus—cohered with the most distant: the Watcher, say, surveying the apocalyptic upheavals in which he could take no part. Marvel Comics were sustained by an undulating web of interconnections. Everything impinged on everything else: to understand where the Avengers or the Inhumans or the Silver Surfer fit into the overall pattern was to get a visceral inkling of the cosmic plan. The individual comic book was merely one element of a kinetic continuum extending far beyond its four-color pages. The implied space in which all past and future episodes were linked was analogous to a higher consciousness. At times, as in the Galactus episodes of *The Fantastic Four*, this consciousness displayed itself openly, with the austere eloquence befitting religious art.

The students thrashed about attempting to define the phenomenon. They sighed, they stammered, they paused to collect their thoughts. It was Dantesque. It was a demonstration of the quantum theory. It was the ancient paradox of the One and the Many, the perpetual oscillation between the unitary cosmos and the ten thousand things of which it was compounded. Each frame of each comic was a molecular cell (further divided into the subatomic elements of line, color, thought balloon) within the all-encompassing monad that might be termed "the Marvel universe."

When you take the microcosmic view, limiting yourself to one frame at a time, you see a world of apparently independent beings functioning within closed groups: hierarchies of complexly interrelating gods (*Thor*), functionaries of the militarist state apparatus whether benign (*Captain America*) or sinister (*Nick Fury, Agent of SHIELD*), the network of telepathic wonder children in *X-Men*, the almost Shakespearian underwater courtiers and betrayers of *Sub-Mariner*. But when you draw back for the macrocosmic vision, individualities are subsumed in larger patterns of movement and line. The literal predicament of the Thing caught in quicksand or Reed Richards changing shape to evade Doctor Doom becomes part of an arabesque. Strictly speaking, neither

Reed Richards nor Doctor Doom actually exists—there is simply an exchange of energy, a turbulence within a unified field. Even the most destructive horrors emerge as necessary compensatory shifts of balance. The annihilating firestorm is an abstractly beautiful gesture. Thus we can say that what happens within the frame corresponds to conventional reality, while the view that embraces *all* the frames, in a detached and simultaneous flash of insight, corresponds to the enlightened mind.

The key to these matters could be found in *Doctor Strange*, the continuing story of an alienated man of the West—criminal, alcoholic, a physician stripped of his license, in short the archetypal egoist intellectual infected with Kierkegaard's sickness unto death— who underwent his spiritual dissolution, his bardo trip, in order to be reborn as a student of lamaistic wisdom at the feet of the Ancient One. This Himalayan guru, a lineal descendant of Sam Jaffe in *Lost Horizon*, had recognized in Dr. Strange the seeds of a perfect master of white magic. (The expatriated Occidental figured as a kind of Messiah, a prophesied god from across the sea, along the lines of the conquistadors.) Eventually, having attained the profoundest depths of *wu-wei* contemplation, Strange spent his days sitting lotus fashion within his tastefully draped and carpeted Greenwich Village pied-à-terre and tuning in to the brainwaves reaching him from across the universe. But while his body sat inert, Dr. Strange's astral form was perennially voyaging, inserting itself into the land of dreams (domain of nightmare), gliding within nebulous mental territories defined by icicles or pink fog, leaping through holes in space and time to save a rarefied, barely conceivable dimension from absorption into the power hoard of the Dread Dormammu.

Here was a Torah apt for every mode of exegesis, an iridescent sutra written in a language of metamorphosing landscapes and bodies in constant motion. This indeed was the living page: not talk about action but action itself. It was so close to the core that everybody could find in it something applicable to himself. Like the *I Ching*, the Tarot, or the signs of the zodiac, Marvel Comics contained all potential meaning, offering scope to every possible reading. Their letters pages were a crossroads where scholars and sixth graders, GIs and peaceniks were linked in a common devotion to the Hulk or Prince Namor.

This arena in which the art of Steve Ditko or Marie Severin could still transcend political barriers represented a last outpost of what was once a unified national culture. Elsewhere the lines had already been drawn. Within the university the various sects clustered in their cells, separated by areas of silence. The groups not only talked about different things; they talked about things in different ways.

The right-wingers, for instance, convened to discuss military strategy—how to keep the Asian flank solid, how to spy on Murmansk—and tell fag jokes. The beer cans piled up until Big Red rose and declared, "Goddamn, I'm gonna put my fist right through that door," and did. He was the same one who said, "Don't get sore, I like nigger music just the same as you," and who liked to rhapsodize about the time back home when they gang-banged the mayor's daughter. He was full of bright gags. "I've got a funny idea—you know the faggot down the hall?" He dragged the guy out of his room, lifted him by the collar, and dangled him for long moments over the tessellated flooring three stories below.

Big Red was a serious student of foreign policy: "Everybody knows Roosevelt sold us down the river at Yalta." His conservative credentials were impeccable except for his merciless baiting of anyone showing traces of religious faith. "You don't mean to tell me you believe in *God* and all that shit?" This was for the benefit of Tim next door, who when not attending math and economics classes studied evangelistic pamphlets. Tim was polite, and clean-shaven, and never betrayed anger when people made fun of his religion.

Not all believers were so placid. A group of sectarians—remnants of a presumably dying tradition—called themselves the Jesus Team and took up battle stations outside the dining hall, poised at all hours for debate on the fundamental issues: the fallacy of Darwinism, the historical reality of Noah, the literal fulfillment of biblical prophecy. They had studied Aristotelian logic in a school somewhere, and were prompt to interrupt an ill-phrased question with "Define your terms, define your terms." Although they favored somber colors and did not smile, they seemed to find a mordant satisfaction in being regarded as sideshow freaks. Their self-imposed martyrdom consisted of enduring the baiting and blasphemies of their doomed classmates.

A more refined Calvinism lingered in the nearby auditorium where a great poet adrift in middle age stared out uncertainly at a solemn audience of literati. They had come to worship at the Church of the Word, a church that could no longer offer anything but sharply etched tremors of doubt and guilt. It was a laconic and half-apologetic funeral service for God. The poet wiped his glasses and muttered into the microphone, neither shouting nor singing nor letting the full force of his voice resonate. The congregation sat respectfully in the pews, with only an occasional cough or twitch to betray impatience. The sermon would be over soon enough. The cakes and soft drinks awaited.

The hush into which the poet's words slid was disturbed by distant yelling. A restless band of youths hammered on the doors of the film club. A Japanese sex movie had been announced. Actually it was just an avant garde short featuring abstract microphotography of genitalia, but by then it was too late for explanations. The campus police went into their riot maneuver. The screening was canceled. The soft-spoken Japanese director stared in amazement at the two hundred boys dispersed screaming across the quadrangle. Even more windows than usual were smashed that Saturday.

Next night was the Frank Borzage retrospective at the cinema club, but there were no rioters: only seven or eight pasty-faced young men gesturing with their cigarettes to describe the Germanic tracking shots of *Moonrise* or the shockingly abrupt cross-cutting that transforms the last sequence of *Mannequin*. And then there was of course *Seventh Heaven*—but that was in another category altogether, among the inexpressibly sublime love tragedies: *Ugetsu, Lola Montes, The Legend of Lylah Clare*. The great directors had repeatedly aimed their cameras at beautiful women (Marlene Dietrich, Anna Magnani, Jean Seberg) and transfigured them: art could go no further than the face of Joan of Arc amid the flames or the vacant stare of the poisoned Ingrid Bergman at the end of *Notorious*, all those monuments of a worshipful gaze on the other side of the viewfinder. There is a heaven in which Rita Hayworth continually descends a South American staircase, and a resurrected Gene Tierney glides through her richly curtained bachelor-girl apartment. To love is to screen the movie over and over, like Dana Andrews getting drunk and obsessively studying the eyes in the portrait of the dead Laura.

But my favorite scene (he said with a wicked smile) is where Richard Widmark kicks the old lady in the wheelchair downstairs in *Kiss of Death*. Or how about the murder in the alley in *Underworld U.S.A.*, or the severed elevator cable in *The Garment Jungle*? The car chase in *The Line-up* is as balletic as the rollerskate number in *It's Always Fair Weather*. The broken barrier and the somersaulting car define the term "action photography." It's so hard to put in words. The filmed gesture is irrevocable, it weighs like a fatality. It's frozen time—an interruption of the universe—but it moves! Not through intellection, only through a kind of prayerful attentiveness can we respond adequately to the moment in *Day of the Outlaw* when Burl Ives gets blown away. It was in any event one of the finest of the later de Toths.

Movies are to be seen. Talking about them is useless at best, intensely frustrating at worst. The discussion can only culminate in a trip to the local nabe. As the boys approach the theater where *A Fistful of Dollars* is showing, their pulses quicken. In darkness, armed with Pepsi and Winstons, they prepare themselves for a vision. The photographic scroll unravels. The plain undulates. The adobe walls shimmer as the camera dollies past them. The vast unshaven face of the heroic killer peers from its bright hermetic world.

The submissive act of watching a movie implies the dominant—and how much more appealing—act of shooting one. To photograph is to master reality, and each element added—motion, color, Panavision—makes the mastery more total. The eye rules. Small wonder, then, that the film directors seem gods. To make *Red Desert*, Antonioni even repainted the landscape. The voyeur as commander reshapes the world into an image of his desire.

To be a filmmaker—that is, to carry around an 8-millimeter Japanese camera and take wobbly pictures of your roommate giggling or your girlfriend staring with passive intensity out the window—was to assume a role in harmony with the age. It was a sacred function: the famous underground film poet had told them so, snarling if anyone uttered, ranting at the brainwashed young bourgeois who had ventured a remark about "boredom." They had been so conditioned to expect a false excitement that they couldn't look at reality. "You're all afraid to see! That's why people like me have to do your seeing for you!"

At the experimental film festival the small screen swarmed with dots and strobelike smears. An arm lifted, again and again. A beautiful girl walked naked into a pond: everyone woke up. The camera lingered on an open wound: everyone looked away. Somehow it was too mechanistic to give them the ecstasy they were hoping for. Watching the underground films, they waited for someone to take her clothes off (except that most of the women turned out to be transvestites) or someone to make a joke about drugs, or at least for some high-speed whirling of waves and particles, an "eyeball kick."

The images—blurred, overexposed, underbudgeted—just couldn't live up to what the words promised. They wanted to see more than any 8-millimeter camera could show—more, perhaps, than even VistaVision or Cinerama could show. They wanted to see the mind itself on the screen, the way filmmaker John Cavanaugh—one of their own generation—described it in the *Village Voice*: "Whenever you move around, everything is so multi-dimensional. If I'm in the woods, like, I have plants up there, millions of spaces that I can move in and out. I have the whole cosmos. Because I have the sky, and the earth, and the water, and the trees, everything. . . . I am interested now in using camera as an energy-transforming machine, to bind kinetic energy sequences. That's to me the important thing, to do this, to bind the kinetic energy. . . . Let's say, I have been taking LSD now, for the last few months, and, according to the Tibetan religions, what it does to you, it liberates the life flux, the swirling energy patterns that make up the actuality of life, and that to me is like pure mind, intelligence."

They could see those spaces between the plants, feel them opening up as he talked. The new talk was like that. It didn't move toward a predetermined end, it didn't make "a point." The old talk screened out the world. The new talk let it come pouring in. You allowed the words to take you into new places, as if a new universe were being created within your sentences: except they weren't quite sentences anymore. They were more an undifferentiated stream of associations, without beginning or end. A stream, that was it. You kept the stream flowing with your talk, and then other people could chime in, and it was like you were all bathing in the same stream together.

It turned out everybody was capable of saying the most incredible things, even psychotics. "I noticed I started to think about slow motion . . . moving pictures . . . why people appear a certain way under slow motion . . . I just began to be interested in the effects of why under slow motion people tend to be . . . why their forms seem . . . they get very massy . . . they seem to have a lot of mass. It seems that you can fit it right into the mathematic model of force and mass and acceleration and velocity and distance . . . as soon as you expand the time element . . . something like distance changes your acceleration." Even if that guy *had* taken too much of the wrong acid, he was still groping toward a kind of truth, *his* truth. "If that's the way you see it, that's the way it is."

When you speak from the center, let it come straight out, then what you speak is truth, expressed in whatever terms are available to you. And then it longer no matters who is talking: having passed a certain limit, you find yourself beyond individuality. Anybody could be the rock musician talking about the word "God" and saying: "I think *energy* is a better word. And that's where it all comes from. It just goes through all those changes and one of those changes it is going through is us—life." There's nothing to add to that, nothing to dispute. Because he speaks from within a place we all inhabit, his statement has a universal validity. We verify it with our own sense of being.

To rap is to construct a paradise. A night of talk is an unwalled and bottomless structure. It starts with someone suggesting that he would like to "stay up all night and really get into things"— "things" being the truths embedded deep inside language—and the next step is someone else borrowing his withdrawn obese roommate's prescription diet pills and passing them around. The resultant tingle emphasizes the *there*-ness of the walls, as if matter itself shivered. In the background something suitably dry and jangling—Cecil Taylor or Karlheinz Stockhausen—further tightens up the atmosphere. The edgy sensation at the back of the teeth changes the texture of reality. Objects are colder and more distinct. The thin boy quotes Bergson on consciousness. In the twenty-first century there will be no art because by then human beings will themselves be art. People standing knee-deep in the godhead—and with no social structures as we understand them—will have no need for "entertainment."

For them the future seemed already to have arrived. It was all part of it: Romilar and Warhol, Ali Akbar Khan and Erma Franklin, the revelatory breezeways of architecture and the novel's hall of mirrors, summers in Marrakesh and winters in the library of the Jung Institute. They populated the room with names. But the radiant structures generated by their amphetaminized brains became inaccessible the instant they were articulated. Those elusive objects of desire—"spirit" and "gist" and "vibration"—slipped away from them like a woman rejecting an embrace.

By the time the sun hit the ivy, all the bracing energy was gone. They were left to stare indifferent at the ashtray heaped with used cigarettes, the Literature of the Enlightenment text lying open where it fell, the *Esquire* photograph of Ken Kesey, whose eyes they had studied in search of some outward indication of higher awareness.

Once again the men had been unable to comfort one another. They had, however, talked a good deal about "love," and had even agreed that "love"—the real one, known to Plotinus and St. Anselm—was the conceptual linchpin joining matter and spirit, the sole binding force, the nut couched in materiality's shell. The fact that "love" was the byword of the day was merely one more sign that this day was indeed different from all other days. The root of being, the diamond-hard heart of Heidegger's *Seingrund* was being laid bare: the time of visions had arrived and they were there to witness it. In the beginning was the Word and, added the Beatles, "the only word is love." Even the diabolist tendencies of the Rolling Stones were transmuted by the prevailing wave of positive energy into "We Love You." Feeling like John on Patmos, they played the record again, having decided that the aural effects in the final chorus offered a stylistic prophecy of the ecstatic cataclysms yet to come.

But there, on that exposed cliff, they stopped. Thus far and no further could they dismantle their personalities. They were destined, after all, to be nothing more than voyeurs of transubstantiation, hypothesizers of rapture. The physical style required by bliss eluded them. Their methodical postures, the elegant but constricted tailoring of their clothes, the fluent wariness of their vocabularies amounted to a resigned acknowledgment of limitations. They sensed, furthermore, that, being male, they were condemned to feel abstract. The most they could stir up in the way of human warmth came from the aggressive energies of argument, the extravagant flauntings of an intellectual mating dance. Tenderness was to be symbolized by a discussion of the purplish gray tones in a watercolor by Paul Klee, or by another playing of the new Temptations record. Indeed, black music seemed to them a reservoir of emotions that they themselves could only point at— just as a figure such as Malcolm X embodied a word like "heroism," which would otherwise have had only a "camp" connotation for them. In a way their whole discussion, no matter what its ostensible subject, was a convoluted, oblique allusion to tears being held back with a sort of casual ferocity. Thus the room full of boys began to seem empty. Nothing was being exchanged.

The last straggler walked disconnected back to his molecular room. Above him hovered, Madonna-like, the specter of a distant or lost or imagined girlfriend: the determining figure of every artwork, the altar upon which his ego was presumably to be sacrificed. The absent woman had the inestimable advantage of being formless and all-permeating, like some etheric fluid. In the bad poems he wrote, she hovered around words such as "dance" and "branch" and "flute" and "shadow"—whatever suggested softness, litheness, darkness. She was both the logical justification for suffering and its cure. The mysterious healer waited in some crystalline niche of the not-yet-come-to-pass to process his complicated bewilderments.

Upon that Botticellian countenance were superimposed the features of the naked girl in *Cavalier*, a magazine that specialized in softcore pornography for frustrated drug users. "Rita digs Zen, Kerouac, and mind expansion. She shares her Haight-Ashbury pad with her cats Mushroom and Morning Glory and a family of free-loving friends. 'Most of all,' says Rita, 'I'd like to have the inner tranquillity of a flower.' " The wet petals clinging to her breasts were a badge of innocence. Nothing was more erotic than purity: with long straight hair and no mascara, she bathed in a rural stream.

As the year moved toward spring, incense sticks blossomed in the night dorms. Smokey Robinson gave way to Otis Redding, the Animals to the Doors. Big Red, the prophet of conservatism, initiated a new avatar with a bundle of purchases: red light bulb, rolling paper, and the latest albums by Jefferson Airplane and the Grateful Dead. The wraparound shades were new, too, although they had the unfortunate effect of making him look like a highway patrolman. He and a few friends were going to "blow some pot." Within a few weeks the whole football team was in on it, passing around joints, giggling thunderously, then closing their eyes to let the harmonies of *Surrealistic Pillow* soak into them. They drew the curtains and turned the strobe on: "Shit, man! I am stoned out of my fucking mind."

By this time the glossy magazines were full of pastel flowers and squiggly lines. The supermarkets began to fill up with eye-popping simulated hallucinations. An army of blond flower girls beckoned from movie posters and soda ads. Sitar music oozed in the background of the herbal shampoo commercial. The esoteric knowledge was spilling out into the exoteric domain faster than anybody could even register.

The elite corps of "heads" went on alert. The integrity of the original insight threatened to founder. The springtime of LSD was decaying into a languid and gnat-ridden summer. Even the visions were wearing out: the purest Owsley, and the chunks of hashish transported by camel out of Morocco and Afghanistan, were not quite enough to sustain an *eternal* high. It was time to go to the real source, to do it the ancient way. Prayer! Meditation! Discipline! Empty mind! Stiff spine! Fasting! Mindfulness! Tighten up your act and engage in ritual purification if you want to be somebody whose every move has an air of inevitability, who—like the extraterrestrial Klaatu—has balanced the forces of the universe within himself and (robe swaying, fingers interlaced in a mudra) glides out to establish harmony by the mere fact of his presence.

Such a being came to see them. The rumor preceded him: the most important event of modern times will occur, unannounced, at eight o'clock tomorrow night. So they enter the auditorium feeling already a certain reverential tremor. In the center of the stage, garlanded with flowers, sits the man from the East: ancient, bearded, white-robed, a wisp of a human, so lightweight they feel they could blow him away by breathing on him. Silence. They become uncomfortably aware of how awkwardly they breathe, how their chests rasp, how nervous they seem to be. The old man looks out at them while the silence deepens: and then he giggles. The high girlish giggle, unmiked, fills the hall. That giggle! Already each of them knows he will never be able to describe it. It is feathery and metallic and has an inscrutably bracing effect on their nervous systems.

Now the silence is even thicker, a palpable unescapable presence. "Tonight I would like to talk to you about the mind." He has certainly chosen the right topic for this audience. His voice is that of someone who would not hurt a fly. They love this man. They would like to take him home with them. "Most people think of the mind as something very complicated. But this is not the case, do you know?" His endearing little wink somehow has the force of an earthquake. "I would like to say to you that the mind is in reality a very simple thing. Not only that, it is also a very gentle thing." Another giggle, eliciting multiple orgasmic ripples at the mere thought of the gentleness of the mind. "So, if we wish to control the mind, it is not by force that we should proceed, but by love and tenderness. We must love our own mind, what do you think of that? Does that sound very complicated?"

He has not once raised his voice or budged from his motionless lotus stance. The silence surrounding his phrases is devastating: the listeners feel as if their brains are being emptied. Is he in fact sitting on the stage, or perhaps a few inches above it? Pretty soon they will all be levitating out of their seats. Surely there must be a way to prolong this sensation.

There is, of course, but it costs thirty-five dollars down payment and abstinence from drugs as a prerequisite. You will receive a syllable, to be revealed to no one, a sound designed for your inner ear alone, uniquely tailored to your spiritual condition by a trained adept. "But how do we know the adepts are as good as him?

Anyway, I didn't like the part about drugs." An enrollment office had been established, part of a worldwide network. Its tone was young, clean, devoid of individuality. The old culture—the culture that persisted in the library's mazes and in the recesses the Puritans carved—had accumulated distinctive crazings, varnished surfaces aged into quirkiness, a gallery of inherited knobs and grilles and heraldic flourishes. That culture died yesterday. The purpose of the new teaching was to neutralize everything into white walls and Formica registration tables and a vase of fresh flowers. Its body of knowledge consisted of the garlanded blowup of the master and, stacked under it, the bound transcript of his lecture series.

Sitting cross-legged on the meditation mat placed in the room's dead center, the enlightened friend focused on the black dot he had painted on the wall. They were discussing some phraseology contained in an underground newspaper: "a state of pure bliss, of ecstatic awareness, a light of understanding which embraces all beings and all things . . . a state of absolute peace . . . a state of absolute freedom, plenitude and certitude, of oneness with the eternal and the infinite." The question seemed to be whether this was a description of an actual state, unmistakable for anything else, or a pointing in the general direction of a dark territory: "They went thataway." "You," said the friend, "may have come to the edge of those words, but you'll never get past that point until you stop regarding them simply as words: that is, until you make a sacrifice. The crude answer to your question is, yes, it is an actual state and, no, it cannot—on the highest level of comprehension—be confused with anything else. But you have a long way to go before such questions are even relevant. You are too in love with your own thought processes, with art, music, all those decorative things. Between where you are now and what you're talking about there is a gulf. Begin, if you want to, by simplifying your daily life. Sweep out your room, make breakfast, sit quietly.

Get rid of your television set—but you don't really want to hear this, do you?"

The effortlessness of his breathing was an unanswerable argument. One no longer pitted argument against argument, system against system: the sole touchstone was physical style, the harmonious interaction of mind and body, the delicate vibrations emanating from lung or larynx, the echo of a chakra or the hazy residue of an astral body. This could not be counterfeited. It was something like a halo, a spiritual merit pin. Magnetic, it drew toward itself a string of precious adjectives: "calm," "loose," "open," "together." Imagine, they would say, what is going on in the spine of that person! Picture the percolations of energy, the rings of light shifting from blue to green to red: power is being manufactured. Don't you wish you could get hold of some of that?

Grasping at Shakespeare or stereos doesn't help. You need to get down to a terribly naked level of bone and fear. Become gristly, ugly, demonic: and if you run from the image in the mirror it is perhaps because you are on "an ego trip," or its subclass "a possessions trip" (the generic American ailment), or—most ominously and irrevocably—a "death trip." This last was the category of the doomed: those who for some ghastly reason—a maimed childhood, a diet too high in animal fats, a self-perpetuating perversity—were incapable of awareness. Not only could they not enter nirvana—at least, not on this spin of the cosmic wheel—but having once inadvertently caught a glimpse of it they would move instinctively in the *opposite* direction, and (it got worse as it went on) would persist in believing they were going in the proper direction. They would call their death "love," would mistake their neurotic hysteria for spiritual experiences, and in the process cause no end of problems for other people. They were disturbed whirlpools of being, sucking everybody else into that nowhere place in their center. "The only way you'll ever get her high," sang Country Joe and the Fish of one such, "is to let her do her thing and then watch you die." Everybody seemed to have known a girl like that. Similar psychic minefields lurked all over, posted like decoys at the very portals of understanding.

God is not simple. Access to wisdom can be unaccountably terminated. The nervous system backs up with contradictory readings of behavior and newspapers. The cafeteria suddenly swarms with spies, rumors, conspiracies. They read minds between the walls. The gift of a book is calculated mockery: I know you have been thinking about this. Guards roam each level of consciousness, disguised as students or doctors. There is a battle between the classroom and the infirmary. I left my mandala in the room and with it, in a sense, my body: at least the aspect of my body that was real. This one is just the casing, the volume. The teeth begin to seem larger than the soda counter. What is to be swallowed looms as a world: a hamburger made of card catalogs and governments. The thing going on in the walls of the ribs has almost burst open the alphabet. The letters bulge at their tips as if an ergot festered there.

The leaves start to go again. The dead tints of yellow and red pile up under the window. The fuzzy rasp of the sitar has a wintry precision. The magazines are filled with accounts of wholeness. People chant by the oceans. Smoke curls from thatched huts. The mountains pulse with newly invented languages. To go outside is to be healed, delivered from the throb of wiring. The complex of educational buildings blocks the light from entering. The graphs are designed for war. The bodies are to be confined. Science tastes like death. Even the smallest manufactured item—a staple, for instance—has murderous implications. A clear mind seeks brine and pollen. An edgeless and unclipped meadow attempts to dissolve centuries of engineering. The turntable switches off. God is simple.

He dropped out at dawn.

THE SCATTERING

It is still early 1967. In fact, it's beginning to seem as if it will always be early 1967, as if such things as years were now ready to melt into the new timelessness. How else account for the oracular accent of the words that are being transmitted day and night? "It's like we all get inside each other's head." "It goes beyond anything that you can talk about in words." "I found out that God is part of me . . . part of everything. I don't get hung up on it, because it's just there. We're really here to have fun; we're just here to groove." "Color is light—and life is color, and music is color. And life and music and color are all relevant to me because love is giving." "You either have this good karma or you don't. And you can always tell people with good karma." "The world isn't going to be straightened out until world barriers are gone. . . . All the barriers have to go down. This must end up being one big place . . . where everybody lives, and works, and people have their own thing." "It's all happening so fast! There's so *much!* Like I just thought of what I said, you know. And suddenly it branched out into about fifty million places. And there are all these other associations . . . all in a flash. . . . I could never articulate them in a million years. They're all there at once! Wow. That's beautiful."

There's a twenty-four-hour wire service from the heart of the eternal present. In some flowered nook of San Francisco—a cloistered space only inches from the external "reality" of America, but shielded from it by home-stitched sacred symbols—someone is improvising prophecies. You hear it on television, on radio, on the street, over the phone, in newspaper and magazine transcriptions. It becomes part of your mind. A thousand separate voices are woven into one, a chorale of raw thought. No transmission has ever been so direct. Half-finished phrases, half-formed conceptions tumble without mediation into public discourse. As we listen to the acid head launching into a sentence that can never end—a dilation of syntax attempting to embody all possible nuances and residual aftershocks of a single moment—we participate in that incompletion with an intimacy hitherto unimaginable. We think *with* him. "Wow. That's beautiful." Nothing inarticulate about it: with the help of such phrases a space is being described, a collective embryo within which a new language can be born. The patriarchal grammar had to do with limitation, closure: its function was to hem you in. The rebellious grammar now taking shape will be liquid, unending, open to anything that needs to speak. In the meantime we must fall back on sign language, body language, the language of grins and glances.

The people who speak this language are recognizable as friends, even though you have never met them, and even though in photographs—snapshots instantly attaining the status of messages from the spiritual front line—there is nothing to read beyond a catalog of artifacts: sandals, headbands, flower-print dresses, blue jeans, yoga pants, a "Sock It to Me" T-shirt. He has a beard. Her breasts are bare. They sleep in a hammock. Their eyes glitter. They inhabit an afternoon that never draws to a close. They smoke joints, lie in darkened rooms listening to sitar music, flash exotic costume jewelry, wave through the camera at the viewer. It is a world without drama, a paradise of trinkets and vegetation and flesh. They sit and look at the ocean. Eventually they will hug. Moving beyond the scarves and rings and painted cheeks of the blond girl in the photograph, your eyes come to rest in her eyes. The gaze caught in the lens is the last barrier separating you from the other side of the gates of Eden.

By now (it is March or April) everyone wants to peer at the newly discovered fauna, to participate at least vicariously in what a French journalist has already described as *les mystères et rites des cérémonies psychédéliques chez les hippies*. Something is going on, right in the pitiless heart of Metropolis. Tribes are emerging from the midst of a terminally mechanized civilization; our parents have mysteriously given birth to their own ancestors. Perhaps some delayed response programmed into the genetic code is just now coming into play, a safety mechanism designed to save humanity from itself. These bands of young hunters and gatherers have come to initiate a new and joyous Stone Age. But the minute they walk into the daylight the trouble starts. The home ground they have scavenged from the old culture's dying cities will now be subjected to various strategies of encirclement, enticement, or outright invasion. Savages are chic, a target for possessive lust. People are looking for the way in, even going so far as to place personal ads in the underground newspapers: "Writer would like to rent acid head or ex–acid head who digs the whole scene. Cool, hip, articulate." "Exciting young man in search of a swinging uninhibited woman for all forms of communication advanced and ultra-innovated." "Creative young couple wishes to meet others interested in painting, Indian and folk music, acid. Object: to join tuned-in circle and/or turn on friendships." There are those who wish to become hippies, those who wish to meet them, those who wish to spy on them.

In the hippie enclaves an air of village intimacy still, just barely, lingers. The natives rendezvous in parks, exchange homemade broadsheets and stews amid the lull that precedes a rough and abrupt plundering. The slowly evolved etiquettes will survive perhaps a few moments more under the new atmospheric conditions, or else will mutate to adapt. The old has come foraging into the nest of the new, eager to suck up its energies. Things had gotten too blatant. The hyperbole of the hippies gave them away: noise and nudity and blinding colors and phrases like "bliss apocalypse." To that hyperbole, as to a mating call, the commodity culture must now respond in its own baying tones: "TAKE A 'TRIP' INTO THE WORLD OF AN LSD SUGAR CUBE! Watch the Hippies Flip-Out with LSD, Love, and the Whole Wild Scene!" For the next six years a Forty-second Street marquee will bear the same unvarying promise: THE INCREDIBLE SEX REVOLUTION. The circus has come to town, digging in for an unusually long stay.

A hippie is no more or less than an authentic human being. By the time anyone grasps this, the species has become extinct, killed— in an extension of Heisenberg's uncertainty principle—by the very fact of being observed. Suddenly a new historic past exists: there were people, there was a city, there was a love so blinding it transformed their names and minds and nervous systems. Last year in San Francisco already assumes an air of legend, accessible only through balladry and megalithic emblems. On the sites where the ancestors' dances were held and their invocations sounded, a second generation lines up outside the free clinic for clap shots and Thorazine, or raises drug money selling back issues of the *Oracle* and the *Barb* to the tourists at Fisherman's Wharf. Robbers and panhandlers stake out the meadows and urban caverns formerly sacred to the great Oneness. Henceforth Love has no fixed location. There is no specific place you can go for it, with or without a flower in your hand. In this diaspora, it's up to each individual to rescue what he can from the dismembered utopia. It was always all in your head anyway; as above, so below; the kingdom of God is within you. The seed of a new Eden has been sown in a thousand, or ten thousand, or a hundred thousand heart-minds. The trick is to keep it alive, to find the little clefts and hiding places where the warmth is guarded.

You parachute into a country without maps. The rule of the road becomes: any visible sign is already outmoded. The flowers that were weapons against state and army now enhance the marketability of toilet paper and deodorants. Day-Glo announces a Mafia-owned tavern. The archetypal flower girl, against a background of Indian cotton blankets and Jimi Hendrix music, goes through the numbed paces of the pornographic loops. If someone says he wants to "tell it like it is," he is probably running for Congress. "Tripster" glasses and strobe lamps are sold in the little mail-order ads in the back of comic books, alongside whoopee cushions and rubber spiders. The only hippies making the papers now are not dancing but dead: overdosed, suicided, murdered. Flowers and wiggly demons from a dead girl's notebook become the first examples of psychedelic art to make it into *The New York Times*. The quickie movies of Roger Corman, Sam Katzman, and Samuel Z. Arkoff—*The Trip, The Love-Ins, Psych-Out, The Hallucination Generation*—are busy converting pastel and paisley shades into basic Supermarket Neon. At the same time the icon of the angelic hippie, that sensitive creature attuned to barely perceptible wavelengths of tenderness, is translated for Hollywood's purposes into either a grunting delinquent (*Maryjane, Coogan's Bluff*) or the effete prey of barbarian motorcyclists (*Angels from Hell*) or, at best, the sincere but confused teenager struggling toward social maturity (*The Young Runaways*). And the drugs—once the only sure guides, the breviaries to which one might turn for instruction—are tainted: the pot has sugar in it, the acid is shot through with amphetamine. It's as if God had been poisoned.

Everybody is alone. A girl in a suburban township swallows something. The capsule promises relation to some larger entity, some Overmind, as though to ingest were to communicate. But the capsule is no good. It merely twists the room into anxious clumps of cloth and plaster. No extraterrestrial voice or face clears the air. She must find a way out of her unpleasant experience by letting a loosely clutched Magic Marker spill its ink into the paper of her diary. Spirals take shape beneath her hand, like traces of an organic process asserting itself *through* her, a sort of possession coming from inside her. She perceives the rags and fringes of her drawing as bushes and winding streams and gnomelike ears. The magenta labyrinth of coils and vibrating dots is using her to make itself visible. She is a conduit for ghosts. Later, when she has come down enough to draw bodylike figures, she will sketch a supernaturally thin woman with straight dark hair and a cowl and long tapering fingernails, smiling as if from a great distance, whose hands extend a goblet. Under this witchy apparition she paints a subtitle, in spectral letters modeled after lightning bolts: "DRINK THIS—IT WILL MAKE YOU WELL." All over America, in similarly isolated rooms, these hidden images are being disclosed. They open one by one, phosphorescent buds nurtured in darkness. The most ancient powers reveal themselves in pictures: the horse, the cup, the tendril-haired enchantress, the serpent, the tower, the molten treasure bubbling out of the broken mountain. In unexpected places—the concert poster, the display window of the secondhand clothing store, the rear door of the van parked by the thruway—the potent eyes of resurrected spirits blink and glimmer.

Real eyes stare back at the painted eyes. Real faces are themselves framed by painted arabesques pirouetting across the forehead and around the cheeks, under the pallid lids and down the nose and cascading into strobelike explosions about the lips. The painted body has been captured by wild tigerish energies. Her face is now a certificate of otherness; her spine and nerve ends ripple; her name dissolves. She will call herself Goblin Girl and wear an onyx pendant in the form of an ankh. In a book on color healing she will find a clue to the powers that seem to flow from her. She and the others of her generation, she will learn, have stumbled upon authentic magic. Diagrams with the potential to kill or madden have been incised, sometimes unwittingly, into doorways and belt buckles. The talisman carelessly affixed to a dashboard can refract soul essence. The turnpikes and benches and motels are anything but what they seem: spirits and images of all sorts, curative or destructive, congregate and wage invisible war there.

You have to find these things out for yourself. You have to find the person who will tell you, who was born for no other purpose than to tell you about them. You are awaiting the precise moment: it may be that when the old man tending the gas pump lifts his head you'll take one look in his eyes and grasp it all. If not, there are other gas pumps. The Road—not the literal highway but the spiritual process enacted on it, and for which it stands—is nothing but a series of occult meetings, concealed messages, forbidding but necessary rituals. The Road is the ultimate challenge. Infinite are the random (but nothing is random) adventures, the accidents (there are no accidents) that befall the astrally serious hitchhiker. Call it karma or synchronicity or the mutual magnetic influence of free-flowing vibrations: the tab of sunshine handed to you by a stranger is predestined, and every casual sexual embrace is the working out of a process begun in another lifetime. Having grasped this, you can throw away your old name and be known henceforth as Peace or Reality or Dharma. You don't choose such a name. It's bestowed on you by the deeper being who lives in the base of your spine and wants desperately to course upward along the backbone to flower finally in your third eye.

With so many enlightened beings walking around, there are bound to be conflicts. If Peace should intrude on Reality's turf, a furious covert tug-of-war must ensue. Those who command most authority—natural patriarchs, born to lay down rules for drifters—have survived hundreds of these psychic battles. Reading an account of how Milarepa zapped the other Tibetan lamas with sheer mind control, they nod knowingly. The way stations of the Road are schools where you learn the purest kind of power, the power that looks like acquiescence, yielding and all-conquering like water, which wears down everything. If nothing else, every guru teaches his followers how to be a guru. Those who have once knelt at the feet of a master may rise another day to try the same trick themselves. There are techniques of ecstasy. Ten minutes of deep breathing can annul ten years of conscious thought. Even an amateur can learn fairly easily to dismantle a personality. It can be as simple as asking an unexpected question. Identities consist of habitual neuromuscular responses linked to a verbal "loop" that repeats a few basic beliefs over and over: "My name is John. I live in the real world. Today is Thursday."

Erasing that tape is only the first step. You need a new narration to fill the space that's been cleared. You are what you think: so you had better select your thoughts with the utmost care. Ideas have medical consequences. Sick thoughts sicken. You begin to realize that the air is full of words that can injure or weaken or misdirect. There are no "minor" statements; every TV commercial is a statement about the nature of the universe. The radio slogans are distorting people's energy, hooking it on car sales and shoe design and illusory politics. The media are broadcasting the sound of a wound and calling it reality. Consider the Beach Boys. All the while they were singing polyphonic hymns of dazzling purity and spiritual concentration, they had suffered from the wild delusion that they were singing about little deuce coupes and no-go showboats. They, at least, were redeemed through the trans forming revelations undergone by their guiding genius Brian Wilson: "My experience of God came from acid; it's the most important thing that's ever happened to me." Now the song can ditch all the *things* that cluttered it—the bucket seats, the soda bottles, the candy-apple lipstick—to openly display its real subject. On the new Beach Boys single the false life of consumerism has been replaced by the direct light of revelation: "Transcendental meditation can / Emancipate the land / And get you feeling grand." Feed your head with words that will put you right, words that approach as nearly as possible the condition of mantra or glossolalia. Sunday nights on the rhythm and blues station, Reverend Dave broadcasts live from Tennessee, puts his hands on the skulls of the faithful, and elicits Godspeak: "Lehooly iliamina goppia lolly alopalo." The exiled hippie tunes in, hungering for a discourse that bypasses ordinary synaptic channels, reaching those parts of the brain ignored by Johnny Carson and Dean Rusk.

Communications that seem to come from outside the system have an intrinsic authority. If it's contrary to what any school ever taught you, then it's probably true. A certain awe attaches to the anonymous pamphlet that displays a crude drawing of a comet gone amok and proclaims: LIFE WAS NOT ALWAYS A TRAGEDY. The mysteriousness of its provenance already gives it the aura of an unearthly herald. We are to believe that a very long time ago people were living in harmony on Earth. This was the childhood of the race, an epoch without so much as the concept of evil. Then one day a comet came from nowhere and practically wiped them out. The horror lay in the suddenness; nothing had prepared them; they were engulfed. In their terror and confusion they instituted laws and religions; like frightened children they built a culture of pain and obligation to atone for their imagined sins. If only they had known that *it wasn't their fault:* it wasn't an angry God, it was just a blind accident. The pamphlet further hypothesizes that if people today can accept that their psychic injuries are only the remote afterecho of a cosmic sideswipe, they might inaugurate a Golden Age of restored innocence. Why weren't we told of this? Because the established powers don't want it known, any more than they want people reading Velikovsky's *Worlds in Collision* and finding out what really happened in history. The official chronicles use "facts" to conceal the shape of the big change we are all part of. They maintain that history happened then, over there. But the true history embraces both the ancient nuclear-powered cities buried in the Atlantic and the flying saucers who hover to announce the impending resurrection of those cities out of the deeps. We measure the accuracy of such accounts by the internal vibrations they set in motion. We feel our way toward their truth, like a psychic running his hands over a murder victim's garments.

An absolute reversal of definitions is approaching, as the Age of Fishes prepares to lay down its cache of knowledge at the feet of the Water-Bearer. There have always been a few people on the planet with some idea of what was in store, but now with each generation their numbers will increase radically. The sci-fi picture *Village of the Damned* was perhaps a prophecy of this advent of the Children of Light, albeit with the paranoid slant we might expect from a product of the moribund Piscean culture. How terrified they must be at the spirit tongues announcing the end of rationalism! They were able to ignore all the earlier portents: the impossible tempests and cosmic freaks documented by Charles

Fort, the Great Airship Mystery of 1897, the message intercepted from Boötes in the late 1920s, the coded communiqués of *Oahspe* and Silver Birch and (most majestically of all) the "sleeping prophet" Edgar Cayce. But the bombardment doesn't stop, it accelerates; we ceaselessly get instructions from dolphins and spacemen and the "little people" we can no longer (in our clouded sensory condition) even perceive. These invisible beings want to help us; they have dictated whole books; they came originally from the earth's hollow interior; their current base of operations is in or under the American Midwest, near where those mounds were built by the lost tribes of Israel.

One can—as indicated in the books of Elijah and Enoch—become a spaceman by "translation." They are eternal; they are in constant communication with one another; probably they do not have separate personalities. Stonehenge was built for them by a vanished race, to serve as something like a radio receiver. They are trying to prepare us for the year 2000. The cities will burn. The coasts will crumble. Not only the books but the memory of the books will vanish, in response to a universal unspoken desire for the purging of accumulated data. Human culture has become a tedious process of writing footnotes to footnotes; the inherited information piles up and crushes us. The only thing left is to sweep it all away. That erasure has already begun, in our minds, where everything begins: by letting all the petty texts fall by the wayside, we make room for a few luminous hypertexts such as the Book of Revelation. A book should not be just another book: it should hold all books within itself. Like the *I Ching*—*just* like the *I Ching*—the syllables retrieved from Patmos seem to harbor all possibility. Events wait, literally *inside* the words, for the moment when they will hatch into actuality. The baleful number 666 is coiled serpentlike in the folds of the syntax of those paragraphs. When the future is unsealed—in all its splendor of demolished skyscrapers and molten shopping malls—we will find that the son of God was born in 1967, most likely somewhere in the Middle East, so as to be thirty-three when the millennium hits.

When your head is in the right place you're wide open to whatever drifts by. The commune-dweller picking berries somewhere north of Mount Tamalpais carries a well-thumbed book (issued by Wisdom Publications, Knoxville, Tennessee) about how the international bankers and socialist politicians are actually agents of the secret order of Illuminati, conspirators descended from ancient Kabbalists and Jesuits: "If you liked *Siddhartha* or *The Teachings of Don Juan* you'll probably enjoy it. I'm not really into politics, but this one's a little trippier than most. It's kind of weird!" In the back of the van, among the rolling papers and the sacks of brown rice, a jumble of artifacts turns up: facsimiles of Egyptian talismans and medieval pentagrams, the treatises of Paracelsus, the Great Key of Solomon, the poems of Aleister Crowley. Hidden truths inevitably come swathed in robes and glimmering pendants and hallucinatory circular patterns. Nothing could be more natural than this resurgence of archaic trappings. The wizard's cap that clings so beautifully to the skull only proves what you had already guessed, that in some sense you *are* Merlin. Each scattered visionary senses that his life is part of a larger mythology; he rescues fragments of it from whatever lore comes to hand, patching together makeshift rituals to give shape to his days. Boy and girl making love are Shiva and Shakti. The marijuana farmer is a new Adam, cradling a shotgun as he names the animals of his Eden. The biker immerses himself in *Paradise Lost*. Resurrected Paiutes from the suburbs tune their voices to the imperatives of the Ghost Dance. Druidic chants and ceremonial geomancy greet the vernal equinox. The casual crisscrossings of a day in the city are plotted and interpreted with the aid of zodiac and Tarot.

A sacred text, whether by Lao Tzu or St. John the Divine or Tolkien or Robert Heinlein, merely clarifies what's already there. You spend all your life looking for the key to the universe and suddenly wake up to find that you're it: that you—stepping from the shoulder of the highway to flag down a passing car somewhere between Phoenix and Tucson, or straddling a surfboard frozen in mid-wave off the Laguna shoreline—are in truth the very Buddha-Nature itself. Here it is! You've come home to the real world, where a mountain is a mountain, man is man, woman is woman, rice is rice. You've gone down to the source of breath, the root of the spine, the microdot in the center of the magic circle. You roll in the grass and let the earth's energy flow directly into you. From the woods comes a whiff of healing herbs. Nature has been waiting for you all this time. You wander deeper in. Outside a log house you come upon a cluster of prematurely patriarchal men, wise beyond their years, stringing guitars, whittling, surrounded by dogs and cats. In the doorway of the ramshackle kitchen stands—naturally enough—the woman. Her flower-print dress is hand-sewn. She comes bearing a heap of food.

This is the woman who waits at the end of the male hippie's solitary pilgrimage. After proving himself through long periods of isolation, of meditation in caves or on mountain peaks, he comes back toughened and purified, a weathered Taoist fresh from the Rockies. All that's needed now is the closing of the circle: he holds half the universe within himself and will unite, inevitably, with the other half. She has until now been incomplete. Only a partnership can set in motion the cycle in which the ecstasy of sexuality leads toward the ecstasy of childbirth, diffusing then into the more muted but nevertheless pervasive ecstasies of spinning, weaving, baking: all those elements of housekeeping which in this context become spiritual acts. Woman is indispensable. She is Gate (initiates the hippie into spirituality), Anchor (keeps him from straying excessively into "far-out head trips"), Amulet (her magical influence protects him from shadowy malevolent forces), Circle (she represents infinity while he represents particularity). Almost imperceptibly she evolves into a Great Dark Goddess, imbued with earth, reigning over the silent and passive mysteries that complement his own bright, active existence. It all has to do with balance. While her man gives exuberant vent to his anger, lust, fear, and jealousy, she smiles wisely and cools out his vibes. She sews astrological patterns into his hunting jacket and unobtrusively manages all the little diplomacies of tribal life which his pride (that rough untarnished manifestation of yang) won't permit him to be concerned with. Inside and outside reflect each other. Just as he, hash pipe in hand, speculates on the structure of the galaxies, she in mirror fashion focuses on the structure of the hearty vegetable stew that the twelve of them will soon be sharing. Everything falls so beautifully into place. Tranquilized by the knowledge that she's in there tending to the energies of the hearth, he sits transfixed in lotus posture on the front porch, improvising interminable modalities on a wooden flute.

After paradise shatters, as it always must, they will carry little pieces of it with them into their separate exiles: mental fragments of the glade where they all became one. The regrets and mistakes are sorted out so as to do better next time. If only Jimmy's girlfriend hadn't moved in. If only those people from the city hadn't shown up with all that speed, or with all those guns. If only there hadn't been that trouble with the locals. If only Fred's sense of family unity hadn't begun to involve various forms of discipline and excommunication, until that dreadful morning when he announced who he really was. When things get too definite they become oppressive. Heaven peters out into rules and grudges. Living free gets to be too much like work. Radiance withdraws from leaves and bushes, until the survivors are left stranded among mute inert objects: stumps, wires, discarded brushes, tools clotted with rust. The Sanskrit letter guarding the barn door gradually wears away, until by the time the county repossesses the bean patch it could pass for an accident of weathering.

But that's what knapsacks were made for. The odors of rot and stasis wash clean in the wind off the night highway. The Road never shuts down. Beyond the forest is the desert. Beyond the desert is the sea. Across the sea are the valleys and mountains where silence itself is the native tongue. From blue rock walls ancient voices echo. Terraced crevasses hide labyrinths of sorcery. The air that sweeps through the passes is hard and clear enough to lay the world bare. A single high-pitched note fills all the space between two peaks. There is where water was first named, and fire, and soil. It is infinitely distant, infinitely near at hand. At the shore of the known world, where the factories drain their poisons into the armored bay, the dispossessed can begin their passage to India.

PERCUSSIVE
MUSIC

The hospital is full of drugs. In the patois of the mad, everything is a synonym for "high" or "agitated" or "police." The patients convene like smugglers in the rec room. Somebody's friend slips joints in during visiting hours. An orderly peddles Preludin to a few trusties. She's ushered into the sunny reception area, puffy from medication, her timing off. She flashes a half-felt smile to her high school friend: "Well, I finally made it to the booby hatch. Don't tell me you're surprised." It's adult to be among prisoners, to share jargon and pills and secret planning sessions in which they overpower guards, rip off employee passes, break into locked medicine chests. ("We could all retire on what's in that closet down the hall.") The gray man with stained teeth knew Kerouac and LeRoi Jones years before they were famous. This is what it is to be on the bottom, to be inside the wards from which the hard knowledge comes. Once your thinking has been certified as dissociative, you become an honorary outlaw, one of the real people.

She writes poems containing words like "lone" and "illusion" along with images of broken hands and broken mirrors. The other patients tell her she is a beautiful person and full of talent. She's learned how to charm the doctors: "It's such a con game, doctors and cops are the same." It's like school, you have to be able to flash the right piece of paper. You try to mesmerize them into putting the X in the appropriate box, the one that will cause the doors to open. They define adjustment as the capacity for obedience; they wag their heads like comically ineffectual guidance counselors. You work toward gaining enough self-control to play their game, parrot the right answers: and then blow it by getting mad, smashing a glass, wounding yourself, and have to start from scratch again.

A day comes when she is placid enough to walk across First Avenue. She wants to talk on the telephone all afternoon: "I've been paroled from the little madhouse into the big madhouse. If I've learned anything, it's that the control setup is worldwide and totally organized; you can't beat it, you can just crawl away from it into one cubbyhole or another. Confront them and they take you apart. And of course they are built into my head, into everyone's head, from childhood, a system of habits and prohibitions which dictates how I talk, what I dream, how I express anger by hurting myself. Basically I'd like to have my head cleared by a wise person—remember the bald filmmaker we met, who'd been to India and spoke Ancient Greek?—and begin all over." First chance she gets, she slips out to get some speed from a guy she knows on Avenue C. She makes a joke about the ex-cons in the movies always looking up their old friends and getting involved in bank robberies.

On the street the radios overlap. Between the pauses in the horn patterns on the Tito Puente record, an expressionless voice describes burning cities: "over a sixteen-block area . . . two killed . . . weapons possession . . . snipers after dusk . . . curfew." Here are empty buildings, too. Burned-out cars surround the radio, which tells of burned-out cars. The holes in the walls are black inviting eyes. The first stirrings of spring evoke an air laden with Methedrine and political violence. "The street is made of metal": this is her idea for a song. She improvises a geography among disconnected dead-white patches: Burroughs, Hendrix, heroin, electronic interference, sheet metal, cold telephone, skin of the paranoid friend. The barrages of telepathy crisscrossing the narrow streets have their remote source in the chemical lakes of Saturn, Neptune, Uranus: any place far enough away to be the home of the fleshless brains, the Intelligences whose pull jerks us around. Their agents wear dark glasses and communicate with one another through invisible subtitles, like the blood-hunting aliens in *Not of This Earth*. The pull—a form of high-frequency radiation—can turn a friend's sentimentality, his love of dahlias and Japanese prints, into a theory of mass murder and conspiracy. "The heat's off": it's those planets again, trying to create a condition in which enormous ice lizards can thrive.

She loves the way the cracks in his face mirror the cracks in the walls, as if—like absorbent creatures in a science fiction novel—they were in the process of *becoming* the lopsided stairwell, the broken lock, the airshaft, the pocked and yellowed floor tiles. Having no other choice, the apartment is relaxed about its apertures: its fire escape trailing off into devastation, its splintered skylight open impartially to sun dazzle and marauders. The bourgeois think they are "real," yet demonstrate the fact by inhabiting elaborately sealed-off spaces. The more solid the citizen, the harder it is to get through his windows. When he enters his home it's like passing through the seven stages of the Babylonian hell-gate.

Down here we are wide open to the roof breezes and the fumes—organic and chemical—spiraling from the stoop. Bodies get knifed inches from the entrance. A friend of a friend—the guy whose stare you found "disturbing"—pushes someone out a window for reneging on a drug deal. The one who set it up in the first place is later found dead behind the gas station. At dusk in the park the talk of blood lends a certain exuberance.

After midnight the neighbors dress like women or cowboys, wave whips and pistols, come shrieking through the door reciting passages from the Bible. The famous piano player says things about white people you wouldn't believe: all the stuff *Down Beat* edits out. Have you ever watched anybody die? Zen guys are tough, not like those cherry blossoms in the haiku books. Bodhidharma would have been more like my dealer: rat-faced, wiry, razor-scarred. After a while you know how to measure the velocity of the body falling across the bar table or the structural dynamics of a professional burglar's suppressed anger. Half the fun of consorting with criminals—I mean the real ones who have killed and been imprisoned, not teenage pot peddlers—is treading delicately along their border lines.

The walk-up apartments are shells within which feelings can rage, can fully flower. The almost empty space shudders with the firestorms of amphetamine dependency, or settles into the junkie's satisfying, thickly forested anomie. Spoon and hypodermic become elements of a voodoo ceremony presided over by the benign pulsations of Charlie Parker, Johnny Griffin, Sonny Stitt. If sounds could kill, all those motherfuckers—lawyers, social workers, record company executives—would be dead by now. As for the Beatles, you can take them back to suburbia where they belong. The heroes are dead or in jail or have been forcibly lobotomized. First they threw him in the drunk tank, then they kicked the shit out of him: permanent brain damage. You want politics, try Malcolm on the Vietcong: "Just a little rice-eating guy in the jungle, but give that cat a blade and nobody can stop him." The avenues and parks and bodegas are strategic points in a condition of warfare. There's an edgy rhythm—coiled like a spring—to which the litany of evasive maneuvers and escape routes has been set. To get the most out of the baseball bat parked behind the door, remember to watch the eyes while following through. Just to show up on the street you have to be capable of giving off murderous vibes.

You think it's different somewhere else, safer perhaps? The zombies on Madison Avenue are inoculated against fear by caffeine and menthol cigarettes. Their bodies are relatively unfeeling, not much different from those of the speed freaks. Their consciousness is devoid of imagery: vacant, they propel themselves from time slot to time slot. If they pause, horror rushes into the silence. Their response to, say, the death of Bobby Kennedy is to compartmentalize the event by taking obsessive note of its trivia— What time did it happen? How long a delay before it hit the wire services? How did Walter Cronkite react?—and thereby repulse it from boarding their reality. Mr. Jones can't deal with physical vulnerability. He focuses on schedules, maps, annual reports, anything that shifts the focus away from the room he is sitting in, the body he is occupying. Being fundamentally paranoid, he is incapable of generosity or sympathy. He desperately looks for human warmth in "clever" advertisements for Tareyton or Colt 45, as if they were proof that the power structure that owns him has a human face. He finds the presence of heavily armed riot police "reassuring" and is certain that neither the President nor *The New York Times* has ever lied. By definition they *cannot* lie, because their authoritative grammar establishes what is real in the first place. The rectilinear paragraphs of the *Times* exude an air of calm durability, like the coordinates of a Roman viaduct. Those hard white delimited sentences—poignant in their neutrality—are ultimate bedrock, a kind of secular godhead. In them the pistol shots, the shriek, the anarchic curvature of the bloodstains begin to be integrated into the framework of the normal.

Anything else is decoration, local color. The Caribbean dancers with bare navels are amusing ornaments appended to that purer inner structure at whose core policy thrust is determined. The exotic landscape containing fellatio and thousand-dollar-a-night call girls is aesthetically pleasing as long as it can be controlled. The executives have their private carnival, and that is proper: their recreational obscenities form a necessary part of an overall rationalist mosaic. Mr. Jones thinks a handful of ionized words— "property," "legality," "security"—will hold the pieces together. If all else fails, the hired guards will whip out their Barettas to protect him. He doesn't even hear the cyclonic winds howling around the pilings of his world.

Fuck him: if he doesn't want to understand, then he won't. He will remain willing to find a phrase like "strategic hamlet" plausible. If he moved any closer to the meaning it conceals, he might start perceiving an ominous glint in the eyes of "his" garage attendant. It is easier, in the end, for him to trust in the articulate assessments of the *cum laude* militarists airing their press releases on "Face the Nation." He's a sad case, this Mr. Jones, a miserable puppet: the longer one thinks of him, the laxer his paunch gets, the more recessive his hairline, the more doglike and defeated his eyes. Intellectually he limits himself to the virtuosity of Harry James, the superior mechanical intelligence of Germans, the seamless efficiency of the kitchen staff at the Rainbow Grill: "They've really got a tight operation going over there." Violence is a marginal uproar. It is reasonable that there should be kickbacks, sweetheart contracts, a Mafia, but not that severed hands should float down the Yellow River or that a dead Nazi should lie in front of the Econ-O-Wash Laundromat.

This is the man against whom the songs are written: the one whose daughter runs off to live in a free-love commune on the Lower East Side, whose son has been arrested while in transit through Akron. Even down here in liberated territory his dispirited presence haunts us. We work hard to forget his language, his way of defining things out of existence. We turn our airy home into a laboratory for manufacturing the new man who will inherit the planet. Our bodies become a canvas upon which weird visions are painted, like something out of Dali or Fellini or Jodorowsky. We come here to burn our memories in the little golden ashtray under the Buddha. We lose our names in the patterns of the Mexican blanket, the brilliant colors of the Krishna poster from the head shop, the Ali Akbar Khan solo uncurling in the cold little pad. Maybe there will be a jug of Gallo or a quart of Bud to go with the tiny square of hashish deposited reverently in the bowl of the hand-embellished Pakistani pipe. The way your thin body leans half-tense against the plaster is an emblem of honesty. I tried to write a poem about you. It's partly in homage to Rimbaud. The first line goes: "Our bodies are a canvas upon which weird Felliniesque visions are painted."

Afterward everybody gets hungry and the girls have to get in the kitchen and cook up a dark indeterminate stew, with brown rice on the side. The alternatives are ordering up pizza from Imperial or actually tumbling out into the night to sit in a booth, read a menu, wait for french fries to come. But they would rather not have to transform themselves: "I'm too stoned to deal with the street, what about you?" Meanwhile, in the kitchen, a can of lentil soup has been discovered on an upper shelf. Now only one person has to duck down for cigarettes and beer and chocolate cookies and ice cream. The evening has begun to open up. Within the safety zone designated by the Indian fabric nailed to the wall, and centered around the low table where the drugs are rolled and measured and spliced, a free discourse can invent itself. Whatever the subject—Ouspensky or macrobiotics or Warhol—it offers scope: they sit around filling in details about the transfigured world where the gods roam.

Hard to imagine that a month later she was dead, arrested, taken over by a "science of mind control." The other one, the boyfriend, got stopped at the airport and is not expected back from Mexico in a hurry. Amateurs: when you go out into the cold air of the world you must be lithe and fast and a good liar. Otherwise the border police will rape you, the FBI will seize the contents of your mailbox, the Afghani mountain men will merely cut your head off and laugh uproariously in their simple-hearted fashion. It takes a street kid's knowledge to beat the odds, rip off the system by fraud or force, and retire to the big lyrical farm in New Jersey with the cow pastures and streams, where the gang will paint and meditate and be a family. Every good criminal wants peace and solitude and quiet labor far from any government. In *Bonnie and Clyde* they inhabit a world of meadows, primary colors, and heart-refreshing country music. They would construct paradise if only the law allowed it.

But the law permits nothing that does not reinforce its own dominance: therefore there will be more walls, more checkpoints, more restricting verbal distinctions. The warden is himself a prison. For him the geometrics of the big house become a way of interpreting the world. Other forms—those that are curvy, spheroid, arabesque—register as intrusions into prohibited air space. Our fluidity enrages them, our fishlike slipperiness. It's our blood they want, our youth, to fuel their cannibalistic superstructure. The induction center down on Whitehall is a mechanism for eating bodies. Their educational system teaches infants to worship the monster that will devour them, to leap gaily into those metallic jaws. It's a form of mass hypnosis: and so, even unarmed as we are, they fear us when we stare them down, they fear that the other designated human sacrifices will start waking up. We penetrate the defense apparatus of the beast with seductive music. We launch a botanical assault. Brandishing our real genitals, we neutralize the pseudo-genitals of the state's weaponry. We astral cowboys steal their cattle, lure their women, burn down the sheriff's office. We hole up in the canyons of downtown and play our outlaw music.

Nowadays, however, the canyon is wired. Our sunlight filters through their chemical fog. We eat their cellophane-wrapped handouts. In an air-conditioned central office far from here, the posse listens in on our phone conversations. They photograph us in the park, compile cross-indexed files of those who are to be eliminated. They own everything: if we escape, it can only be aboard their bus, their train, their jet. The money has their name on it and we are not allowed to invent our own money, just as we are not allowed to invent our own prophetic speech or kinship structure or tribal code. The television eye of the corporate rulers scans the settlements for unauthorized wavelengths.

At nightfall their massiveness oppresses us. We dream of being lighter than air, shadowless, with a false name, a false passport, an assortment of private languages in which to contact the other members of the resistance. To defeat the CIA, think like the CIA. Plug into the grid of global interconnections and try not to panic at what comes rushing into your consciousness: enforcers, torturers, secret armies of mercenaries, diabolical scientists working overtime beneath the Rockies, warehouses of mind drugs and bacilli awaiting consignment, spy satellites, laser beams, weather war, international combat waged among telepathic assassins.

Emerging into the already archaic technology of Broadway after the opening of *2001*, we felt so small, so threatened by the coming science. In our fragile isolated bodies we represent the last generation of natural humans before the era of mutants and robots and computerized intelligences begins. The free thought we revel in is about to be drowned out by the stronger signal emanating from the electronic center. In the movies they show in psychology classes, of people with electrodes implanted in their brains raising or lowering their arms at the command of an unseen researcher, we see the crude preparatory stages of the main project of the twenty-first century: the dismantling of the individual. Whether for good or evil, the inevitable homogenizing of separate minds into a fluid generalized medium is the only conceivable alternative to the self-destructive war culture inherited from Aegean pirates. Our own localized skirmish with the ego's dominion is but a brushfire in that larger holocaust about to sweep away the inherited categories.

When we let our identities go, like we did the other night, we get a small foretaste of how that future mind will *feel*: a warm circuitry luxuriating in its own internal crisscrossing pulsations. The electronic rivulets both send and receive, fertilizing each other. Material objects—less substantial now—bathe in the pervasive psychic ocean. Like a mantra dissolving verbal thought, the nonspecific ether of unleashed mind will melt away nations, grammars, selves. Then will come the wide-open transparent streets and gauzy cities of *Slan* and *Dune* and *The City and the Stars*. Great banks of stored feeling will impart wisdom on essentially the same principle as a vending machine: except that by then money will have been replaced by spiritual power. The magicians will reign.

But amid the poisonous waste of Forty-fourth Street the pure screen begins to swarm with ravenous black dots. A molecule of venom corrupts the crystalline point from which all ideas are born. We had forgotten for a moment that the police own science. The first selves to go will be ours. They're coming to get us. It will be so easy to find us in our various ghettos, to flush out our last hiding places, to erase even the memory of us. We *are* Vincent Price in *The Last Man on Earth*, about to be slaughtered by the new race of vampires. How could we have expected to get out of the twentieth century except through its traditional routes: massacre, bombardment, systematic genocide? How could we have expected to build a culture in the shadow of their silos?

We have been naïve, and it is perhaps too late. We can only sound the alarm. All the witnesses in the Oswald killing have vanished or changed their testimony. The medical records were altered, the films confiscated. The diplomat's heart attack was induced by injection. With their army of CIA hirelings they can do anything. They're coming to get Ginsberg and Dylan and all of us.

The stormtroopers and concentration camp doctors are in place. The Frank Zappa song "Concentration Moon" is not a joke but a warning. The systems of registration and incarceration have been ready for decades. The ruling elite moves imperturbably toward total control. They have already killed Malcolm and the Kennedys and Martin Luther King. I know this for a fact. A friend whose father works for one of the more arcane branches of the Pentagon called him up in March to alert him: Get out of New York or any other major city before the first of April. There will be violence, riots, enormous destruction. The streets will burn. No, I can't tell you why; but you are my son, after all. On April 4—only a few days off schedule—Martin Luther King was gunned down in Memphis. The streets burned. Out on the beach on Long Island we gazed at one another in wonder.

The air gets so thick with bad news that it begins to feel like the hospital. The blinking corridors are watchful. The impulse to cower like a hunted animal shakes the body, humiliates it. Impotent hatred of the police surfaces as a numbness at the fingertips.

We should have done target practice long ago. We should have gone across the ocean or into the hills. The brutality of their sexual responses has irrevocably warped the narrative structure of history, and our nests and gardens are not strong enough yet to resist. My bones are sore with fear. I don't want the radio to continue, I'm afraid of what will come from it. The crowds disperse, the parks empty, the plazas go silent with suspicion and dread. The cover of the underground paper this week is not rainbow but black: love is over. The real stuff has begun. Notice how the music has become as abrasive as possible. The feedback disturbs the narcotized contemplatives. Lone gunmen and slashers proliferate like punctuation marks in the larger text. It is not a pretty story, not a story whose ending anyone is particularly anxious to hear. Intermission time was more fun.

In this context amphetamine resembles a barricade of static that shields us from news whose import we have already intuited. Make the present moment so busy, so overloaded, that the future is permanently pushed back. Finally even the present disappears: *They can't get me if I'm not here.* When you smoke a cigarette nothing is happening. The realization of actual existence is perpetually deferred to the moment *after* inhaling, but by then you are already beginning to conceptualize the next puff. I've come to like that nervous absence of space. It harmonizes with the imaginary country where the radio voices live. They, too, are always at a distance: the news happened somewhere else. Destruction is never quite at hand, it merely brushes against neighboring crevices. We are almost as well protected as a man in a space capsule.

Insomnia is indispensable. In its landscape of smoke and bare bulbs, the desensitized body becomes all the more palpable: a blind hammer striking against time and space until the cracks show. Be a fast car. Bruise the nervous system until it resembles the televised jungles of Indochina. Throbbing scar tissue has its own vitality. In a song, if someone sings the word "dead" a jolt of energy comes across. Similarly, the culture of gasoline and knives and cheap wine is a hymn to life. The scholarly young man walking out of the Lyric at midnight, having immersed himself in the battering and convulsing bodies of *Angels from Hell*, feels cleansed enough to say: "I love violence." The kitten will be named Adolf, by way of coming to terms with annihilation. "To have done nothing that was not done for kicks." They have stood on the brink of such an epitaph and admired its icy purity. As in the Godard movie: "Lovers love, killers kill." The guitar solo is *evil*. Survival in this climate will henceforth require the adoption of reptilian characteristics. Tough and slinky, we'll weather the laser wars. Hitting our arms with needles is a way to get in shape for it, an Apache ritual gearing us up for the approaching massacres.

AMERIKA, AMERIKA

There had been a country called America. Although it was lost to them—all the more utterly for having never existed—they were left with a persistent unappeasable craving for its numinous sandlots and hot dog stands, for the splendors of its Wurlitzer organs and the exuberant precision of its dance teams. For years they had dwelled among its ten thousand artifacts: Zorro cards, Westinghouse refrigerators, "The Polly Bergen Show," the interminable chronicles of Nancy and Sluggo and Little Lulu, the theme music from "Victory at Sea," Aunt Jemima and the Morton Salt girl, the Purple Heart, the Lincoln Memorial, Mister Wizard, Howard Johnson and his twenty-eight flavors, James Cagney, Debra Paget, Old Faithful, Old Ironsides, the red and green lights of Christmas. A landscape of faces winked back in recognition, faces from an endlessly cross-referenced album of cousins and uncles. Each of the various constellations—television stars, military heroes, the Rheingold Girls—spoke of an uncanny oneness underlying the profusion. All the images America had ever made of itself came together in the most splendid fireworks ever seen. A homemade love lit up the night sky.

The magic required undifferentiated assent. Say no to any one of the pictures and they all died. There remained a heap of painted grimaces, smudged photographs, mildewed back issues of *Life* and *Movie Secrets*: mementos of a peculiar place where things happened by consensus and everybody laughed at the same jokes. Even in the old days, of course, they had heard rumors of history. The man in the barbershop let on that Eleanor Roosevelt was a Stalinist agent, and that Truman should have been impeached for not letting MacArthur drop the H-Bomb on China, the same MacArthur who should have stepped in as Truman's replacement except "they wouldn't let him." On the school bus a poster exhorted: Stand Up and Be Counted in the Fight Against Communism. Local kids came home from Boy Scout meetings mysteriously changed, their conversation sprinkled with references to the Soviet Menace.

Politics, in the long, well-fed slumber after the war, existed somewhere else. An action-packed adventure story unfolded on a screen, narrated by Quentin Reynolds or Walter Cronkite. Crowds surged. Leaflets were torn to shreds. A voice screaming "exile" and "homeland" radiated from a podium. Zealots smashed windows. Conspiracies sprang up. A leader wearing dark glasses was shot dead in his car. The authentic political spectacle—the kind that happened overseas or south of the border—was as violent and as structurally satisfying as a sporting event. Mostly it had to do with the rise and fall of kings: King Hitler, King Stalin, King Batista, King Trujillo. Seen from a distance it formed a geometric pattern, a ballet of shifting centers interspersed with gunfire. The same episodes popped up with reassuring regularity: the scene where the dictator is trapped in his innermost headquarters, the scene where the troops revolt, the scene where they tear down the statue in the plaza, the scene where the triumphant conspirators begin to turn on one another.

Such things impinged on America only as a disease-bearing virus might threaten a healthy organism. Immense hermetic brotherhoods—the FBI, the Secret Service—served as a defensive ring against incursions. Of necessity they functioned a bit differently from the rest of America. While the civilian nation relaxed at soda fountains or lolled among bleachers, ready to extend a "hiya" to any random stranger, the watchdogs unobtrusively patrolled the margins. Their job was to stare ceaselessly into the crowd until they found the ones who didn't belong. An apparently average Joe might easily turn out to be a Joszef or a Yossip cunningly educated in the local lingo. First in Berlin, and afterward in Moscow, trainees sat in cubicles memorizing baseball statistics and radio gags and the measurements of Hollywood starlets. As soon as they could pass for soda jerks they came to America. The trick was to tag them before they blended in. But they weren't to be arrested immediately; it made better sense to track them with walkie-talkies and two-way mirrors, feed their radio codes and fingerprints into a centralized filing system, let them unknowingly betray a whole network of sleeper agents.

The naïvely trusting nature of the average American—bred to freedom and scarcely able to imagine its absence—made him uniquely vulnerable to alien contamination. It was hard to make him understand that a gas station attendant could be a spy, or that Brooklyn might be the nesting ground of a secret army. For that matter, there was no need for him to be troubled by such matters. The police could do his worrying for him. Whatever uneasiness he felt could be exorcised at the movies, through science fiction fantasies of man-sized insectlike creatures hunched over the control panels of ovoid space ships. The invasion force transmitted telepathic messages to hypnotized subjects: a rookie cop, a bus driver, a manicurist. These were mere pliable zombies. More dangerous were the liberal scientists, who seemed to actually *like* being taken over by the aliens, and would deliver long speeches about how much humans could learn from the intellectually superior extraterrestrials. There was nothing they wouldn't betray. Before long they were eluding security guards in order to rendezvous with the spacemen at a landing site near the Potomac, ready to assist in the final takeover.

America with a *c* was that zone of passive innocence not yet penetrated by Venusians. Its politics were about the absence of politics. Freedom's survival depended on nothing ever happening. The public text must not be too specific, and anyone attempting to particularize it would be apprehended. The Communists, for instance, had been removed from Hollywood because they interpolated references to labor unions into Betty Grable musicals. Nouns had extraordinary power, and many could not be used at all. The existence of the word "virgin" became the basis for a legal battle. Such words had to be fought for one at a time, like Pacific islands in the last war. Meanwhile the standardized speech of Dwight Eisenhower or Bob Hope persisted, an exercise in negation skirting the not-said by means of increasingly sophisticated evasive patterns. The discourse of consensus could endure only by not meaning too much. Subject matter was the enemy: an enemy whose inroads were blocked by an invisible shield of bleeps and delayed-signal devices. At all costs the screen must be kept under control. Political ideas could be expressed only through simile, and so it was the golden age of cowboy movies. Ranchers and outlaws and ambivalent sheriffs circled around one another like the subclauses of some dark and troubled dialectical argument. Through cowboy movies the raw facts of politics—lynchings and rebellions and expropriations—were safely relegated to an alternate America, a nation of the mind, the only one in which events were permitted to take place.

Yet things did happen. Word crept out. Cities were taken over, political opponents killed, senators and ministers paid off or intimidated by disciplined legions of murderers. They got Portland. They got Kansas City. They got the docks, the trucks, the bars. They called themselves businessmen. They called themselves union leaders. They wore dark suits, held meetings in the back rooms of novelty shops, made millions passing around vials of white powder. Above all they tortured people—exotically, with a live wire or a blowtorch or a hearing aid turned up too loud—and if that didn't work they killed them. Children's bodies were flung across suburban lawns. Crusading newspapermen were fished out of rivers. Skulls were smashed over questions of jukebox rental, while apelike rack jobbers beat up elderly shopkeepers. The story was told again and again, in *The Phenix City Story* and *Miami Expose* and *Inside Detroit* and *Chicago Confidential*: a movie for every city, all of them alike.

The gangsters perfected an assembly-line fascism, deploying their enforcers and vice rings as nonchalantly as if they were mass-marketing cheeseburgers or station wagons. No one could go up against Corruption City and live. Fear ruled its streets. In the movies the turning point came when someone—Barry Sullivan or Cornel Wilde—was pushed so far he lost the fear of dying. The sight of his father's grocery store in flames or his wife's Packard fragmented by a car bomb became a catalyst for civic revolution. A collective righteous fury swept the mobsters away, until after a final savage hand-to-hand struggle the hero had the king of the rackets at his mercy. His hands would begin to close around the hated neck until a priest or lawyer or other agent of civilized values restrained him: "I know how you feel, Tom, but don't you see that if you do that, you'll be no different from Vincenzo?"

A benign reformist regime was presumed to come into existence just after the end titles. It would be led by people looking very much like the members of a surburban school board. The world they initiated—a world of carefully observed zoning regulations, of elections conducted in an atmosphere of dignified boredom— represented the final expulsion of violence from the body politic. "We don't do things that way anymore." The boredom was a proof of democracy, and the fact that all the candidates looked and talked exactly alike reinforced the sense of hard-won harmony.

Nevertheless there was a fracture. Much as the PTA and the Chamber of Commerce wished to constitute the whole of reality, they remained only a part. They had succeeded in making Main Street look quite neat. The library's façade had been scrubbed. The recently opened shops sold books, flowers, cards. But no matter how many reformers were in place, they hadn't accomplished more than a holding action. The mob lived just across the highway, in truck stops and brothels announced by distinctive neon calligraphy. It was simply a question of knowing where the lines were drawn. Police kept the peace between the adjacent realities of downtown. The villages enjoyed a liberty demarcated by holsters. There was hardly ever any trouble. You had to learn which places to stay out of.

The farther out or down you went the more ominous it got. It was a country of fiefdoms guarded by bull-necked sheriffs and snarling attack dogs. An implicit threat of violence warded off any impulse to jar that feudal stasis. Every inch of ground was owned by somebody. Small boys were warned against trespassing. There had been a problem about broken windows: "Next time I'll press charges." Looking in the eyes of the man who owned the parking lot, the kids came upon something inflexible and unforgiving. The landscape of property was scarred with glacial stress marks. A trimmed hedge might be as harsh as a fence. The boundaries had been established a long time ago. Nothing could shift them, nothing but money—and the money was all in private hands.

The armored vigilance of the towns was mirrored on a headier scale by the missile depots of the central government. The nation was ruled from within unbreachable cement headquarters. Its gold—the heart of its strength—was safely sealed in Fort Knox. America had, and would always have, more toys than any country on the block: more wheat fields and minerals and airplanes and bazookas; and what it didn't have it could buy. It could crush anything, but it didn't. It didn't need to. Its mere presence was a threat. The very title of the President of the United States weighed like Death or God. He didn't just have bodyguards, he had the whole Secret Service, a government within a government. No king had ever been so well protected. His body pulsated with the power converging on it. The stiff white buildings of the capital were weirs for trapping and holding that power. As he stood framed among them he bathed in what had been captured.

Whenever the kids retraced their route they ended up at that particular crossroads: the dead body of Kennedy precipitating in its fall a shorting out of networks within networks. So much had been hooked up to a single point. The interval of fumbling in the unexpected dark was brief—order was restored with astonishing speed—but the tremor didn't go away. Once the continuity of the show had been broken even for an instant it could never regain its unquestioned plausibility. It was as if the star of a TV series died and his role was taken over by an understudy: "You mean they were actors all along?" No replacement could be fully real. Henceforth the world spectacle would seem aggressively false. The script sagged; the substitute actors repeatedly stammered or missed their cues.

The split second when the connections were severed had been an education. When the picture was restored they could see it was a front, had always been a front. The visible part of government consisted of formularized camera setups jazzed up with a few cheap special effects. Hubert Humphrey or Stuart Symington quoted Jefferson and Franklin D. Roosevelt within a static rectangular composition, while behind the oilcloth backdrop the gangs ruled. There might even be a man with a gun standing just out of camera range, to make sure the speeches were broadcast as scripted. The gangs had wanted Kennedy dead. Evidently the President had begun to imagine that his borrowed robes really belonged to him. The bosses had put him in his place, scarcely bothering to conceal the traces of their act. (The transparently incredible "single-bullet theory" could not be called a cover-up; it was more like a contemptuous admission of guilt.) Now the gangs wanted war in Asia and the murder of civil rights leaders. Public policy obediently mirrored their secret agenda. Power had never been visible in America, only its puppets. The precincts of the gang leaders— the oil barons and the generals and the stockpilers of real estate and weaponry—were closed to outsiders.

Democracy had evolved into the most sophisticated con game in human history. The political parties that periodically put up candidates for reelection represented little more than rival PR firms, competing for the big contract from the military-industrial complex and its Mafioso henchmen. The congressional charade was an exercise in calculated wheel-spinning. Freedom was permitted as long as it didn't change anything. The television industry helped keep spontaneity to a minimum by hooking everybody on a hypnotic sequence of verbal and visual cues: "Don't look away. The important part is just coming up." It was *Triumph of the Will: The Musical*, an endless variety show celebrating the passage of time, interspersed with commercials for furniture polish and menthol cigarettes.

Behind the screen the network people guarded the image vaults.

It was their job to select what the public would be allowed to see—in consultation, that is, with the politicians and industrialists who paid their hire. Thousands of artisans worked day and night to maintain the biggest lie ever constructed: Amerika, a multi-media happening modeled on the World's Fair of 1939, a hall of mirrors with a vending machine in every corner. The media colluded to sustain an illusion of three-dimensionality. Meanwhile, in the airtight central precincts, the permanent secret government went about its business. Its business, this time around, was to consolidate the crumbling edges of the empire. Its chosen method was genocide.

The young people began to recognize that they had been born into the innards of a gigantic and destructive machine. It carried them along with it on its maraudings. They had no control over where it was going, and they couldn't attack something that was all around them—something of which they were part. If only they could slow it down or make it stop altogether! Perhaps if enough people got together they could simply jam up the works. But first of all they had to separate themselves from the monster that had spawned them. They needed to stand outside their own origins. After all, they had never known anything but this long brightly lit schoolroom lined with portraits of Washington and Lincoln and the Pilgrim Fathers: ancestors whose benevolent gaze now hardened into bare blind rock. The old republic, if it had ever really existed, had been supplanted by a breed of ferret-eyed Caesars, pitiless technocrats whose notion of warfare was to dump tons of corrosives on randomly selected villages.

"I can't believe this is happening in America." At school they had talked like that about the succession of killings and small-scale civil wars. But the America of which they spoke had been an optical illusion to begin with. Now that the concealed ghettos were exposed (by flare light) to television cameras, they could see where the roads led. Follow Elm Street to Eastern Boulevard and make two rights and the pavement began to crumble, the pipes ran dry, the law stiffened into an army of occupation. Another language was spoken in those parts. Malcolm, for one, had provided a key to its syntax and transformational rules. Words that had become hollow—"struggle," "courage," "liberate"—were to be restored to their true meaning by any means necessary. The exhilaration of demolished masonry suggested a new kind of freedom. Breeze rushed through the shattered culverts to aerate the city's clogged channels.

Something had to give way. This particular movie had been going on long enough. The establishing scenes of sterility and oppression had made their point. It was time for the assembling of the folk army, its training on rough campgrounds, its songs of hope and yearning, its first skirmishes, its final triumphal march. The only question was what sort of army this would be. Various portents hinted at a mystical nonviolent revolution, a worldwide sit-down strike, a swelling band of unarmed apostles. Sheer numbers might overwhelm the state's machinery. Love attracts love: here perhaps was the long-sought principle that once and for all would break the historic cycle of violence—and thereby end history. Aggression had no defense against universal pacifism. "First we draw everyone—or at any rate a critical mass—into a spiritually unified group. Then we all refuse. The system will stop." The sight of civil rights marchers on television had suggested that the millennial beating of swords into plowshares was both practical and imminent.

A crowd was a form of melting. They were marching against the obsessive rigidity of the Rusks and McNamaras, the tight little men with their graphs and strategic analyses, ready to kill by remote control while sitting unmolested in boardrooms and luxury suites. The folk army rose against murder by numbers, against that Reign of Quantity that signified the terminal desiccation of the West. The function of the crowd was to dissolve the dried-up trash of the old world and moisten the ground for new shoots. The peace marchers moved like the Taoist conception of water, utterly passive and utterly unstoppable. Within the crowd an extraordinary warmth and openness flourished. It felt like the regathering of a scattered family. Here, for instance, were the Communists, the survivors of the old party: and they were lost grandparents, their faces weathered by suffering, marching side by side with a bunch of long-haired, flower-bedecked kids. Government spies took note of everything, and months later a photo of the group would turn up in a right-wing newsletter: "As this picture indicates, hippies represent a new and ripe target for Communist subversion."

For many of the younger participants, the peace march offered a first taste of power. Being part of a crowd triggered a chemical change. As they moved through the downtown streets toward the induction center they felt wide open as never before, part of a collective heart. The surging monosyllabic chorale—OUT NOW, OUT NOW—was like Bach raised to the hundredth power. They did not so much listen to that music as become it. They wept at the joy of it. Together they were infinitely strong, infinitely resilient. The construction workers hurling eggs at them from the scaffolding would one day join them. The inductees, too, and maybe even the cops, would ultimately—like at the end of *Potemkin*—recognize a common humanity and come over to the side of the rebels. Only the spies and informers, those irredeemable butt ends of the fascist personality structure, would be left to crawl back defeated to their bosses.

The march was on television. It was a confirmation that they had participated in history. That the event was photographed made it real, even if the official crowd count was absurdly low.

As they scanned the footage they couldn't help looking for their own faces. It didn't matter, of course. The crowd itself was them. They were getting used to such representations, but the kick was still there. When they saw a TV interview with any given hippie or pot head or peacenik it was essentially like seeing themselves up there on the screen. In fact it was disappointing if they didn't appear. Being part of this generation was a little like being a movie star: "I was on CBS tonight." "I made *Look* last week." They had all (billed as "Americans Under 25") already been chosen as *Time*'s Man of the Year. As with any star, however, staying on top required keeping up a steady flow of new material.

They could not help observing that the war was still going on. Every night the footage of smoke and rubble and the recitation of body counts continued, while they sat watching it in a world invulnerable to mortar fire. The spectacle numbed them. They had to keep reminding themselves that the flat pictures—wedged between Alpo commercials and summer reruns of "Hogan's Heroes"—pertained to irreversible deaths. "I can't believe it's still happening. They *have* to stop it pretty soon." Something would change. Johnson's advisers, after watching the protests from a balcony, would take him aside: "Sir, they're just not buying it anymore. I'm afraid we have no choice but to pull out."

But the change wasn't coming fast enough. It would take more than peace buttons and chanted slogans. The powerful vibrations that had been unleashed in the march on the Pentagon—a mustering of all the energy the underground had to offer—were lost on an enemy insensitive to anything but the grossest applications of force. For the pigs to get the message, it would be necessary to hit them where they lived. Commando teams were better suited than crowds for such tactics. One morning the newspapers announced that the induction center—the very one they had marched against—had been reduced to ashes by unknown arsonists. The counterescalation had begun. It was hard not to applaud the lone outlaws harassing the flanks of the beast. Their very existence enabled many to inhabit—vicariously—a new Sherwood Forest. Identifying with such exploits entailed no risks: "Hey, that's one up for our team."

Everybody knew who the enemy was—without fail he showed his face on television every night, in the form of President Johnson or General Westmoreland or General Hershey or some other Official Spokesman—but it was somewhat harder to envision what would happen after the enemy had been knocked off. Somewhere there must be a different kind of country. They glimpsed it in the face of Ho Chi Minh, poet and strategist and father of his people, an icon more Lincoln-like than any living American. The sorrow and wisdom in Ho's eyes spoke of a place worth dying for, a tropical egalitarian state at once tough and tender. At its core was a protective community where women and children could live in peace, where human worth counted for more than shaving cream revenues. To contemplate a landscape in Cuba or North Vietnam was to feel more real. After the mirrors shattered it would come to this: a field, a road, a child, a worker. Where late capitalism was shallow and disputatious, the emerging socialist culture would be deep and harmonious. People would no longer be divided against themselves. They would not waste their lives on the treadmill of consumerism, isolated image junkies sustained by the glow of a cathode ray tube. They would touch wood, mud, stone. They would work for one another. Slowly casting off implanted ego games, they would recover the rhythm and feeling tone of the truly human.

Mao-Thought, with its broad untroubled aphorisms, was a harbinger of that world: "Serve the people." "Go to the people." Each such phrase opened a pathway into meditation. You did not "read" it, you ate and drank it: once absorbed into your breath and bone structure, its implications shaped your every gesture. Your heart would become as spacious as a plaza in Peking. Anyone seeking to transform the world must first transform himself. In that sense it was like being a Buddhist. Che Guevara might be a monk of a new discipline, a contemplative master for whom thought and action had finally become one, in a unity that resolved all paradoxes: "We must hate our enemies with a revolutionary love."

Che's face alone—framed over countless beds and couches, plastered on walls, miniaturized on buttons—fascinated by its formal perfection. The glance was dry, luminous, agile, focused: the portrait of a supremely centered human being, a man who would hold nothing back in any of his actions. There was something balletic about being a revolutionary. Stylistic grace reflected political clarity, as Abbie Hoffman implied: "The Vietcong attacking the U.S. Embassy in Saigon is a work of art." The improvisatory coiling movements of guerrilla warfare suggested an aesthetic of pliability and flow, as against the mechanistic stiffness of the U.S. war machine. While the blind juggernaut raged and stomped, nimble revolutionaries ducked under and around and between.

The generals were humiliated. The ministers of state continued to issue their usual press releases: "What has been done by the splendid Americans who are there has already yielded dividends of historic significance. Behind the shield which we have helped to provide, a new Asia is rising." Watching an exhausted LBJ withdraw his candidacy was like tasting blood. Something was getting through. Maybe the young people could pull it off. There were so many of them, and the old were visibly losing their grip. New converts were coming over every day from the far side of the generation gap. Even in the official rhetoric the fault lines were widening: there was a kind of sadistic fun in watching the spokesmen squirm and retract and stall for time. Meanwhile, on city walls a new phrase was displayed: SMASH THE STATE. Maybe—

if they could only figure out where to position the chisel—they would succeed in doing just that.

Since the state was top-heavy, the practice of revolution within its borders became a kind of judo exercise. "We'll blindside them, get them off balance, let their own weight take them down." The Man was so keyed up about Russians and Cubans that he hadn't considered the possibility of being jabbed in his soft underbelly. The middle-class revolutionaries had initially enjoyed the benefit of surprise, and the Man was still reeling. Even now that he was alerted, the advantage remained with the rebels: that is, with the Man's own children. As one underground communiqué put it: "We are behind enemy lines. We are the sons and daughters of honkiness. We are going to wipe out the imperialist state and every vestige of honkie consciousness in white people. Our military strategy takes into account our ability, because we are white, to be everywhere; above, below, and within the belly of the pig."

The pig was everywhere, and everywhere the same. Reports flowed in from all over the country: a pregnant woman beaten in Washington, an unarmed demonstrator shot dead in Berkeley. "The S.F. Tac Squad and California Highway Patrol are freaked-out brutes." Learning to hate wasn't hard. The hate fed on re-iterated images of clubs and helmets. The goggled eyes of the riot squads epitomized a closed-off perceptual system: "The police are terrified of seeing or of being seen." Here, armored and ready to kill, were the storm troopers about whose neural responses the students had so often theorized. An alien army in shiny protective uniforms converged on street demos and student strikes, at the behest of ostensibly liberal mayors or university presidents. At this point—as the sun glinted off the guns and the canisters and the robotic headgear—the real Amerika at last came into view. Had the strikers imagined that they might be exempted, that the civilian administrators might intervene on their behalf? If so, they had misunderstood the options available to the bureaucrats. "If you refuse to recognize their authority, they are forced to use the only power they have—pig power." The think-tank boys were at the mercy of their own goon squads. The frightened articulate grown-ups—the ones who quoted Matthew Arnold and preferred to think of themselves as *humane*—crept away to make room for the frightening homicidal grown-ups.

There was no pity in the eyes of the enforcers, only an impersonal ferocity anxious to make a clean sweep of any unanticipated human complexity. This was emerging as a distinctive Amerikan approach to interpersonal relations. Charles Whitman randomly picking off students from a campus tower, or Lieutenant Calley simplifying the jungle through massacre, or Johnson and Nixon plotting genocide with pins in maps: all partook of the same profound impulse to delete. The celebrated acknowledgment that "we had to destroy the village to save it" summed up a philosophy of salvation through erasure. The Bomb stood in readiness as the ultimate cleanser, a white tornado to eradicate the stains of undesirable ideologies or dialects or hairstyles. Within the militarist mind, the nuking of Hanoi beckoned like an outwardly enacted satori.

The Amerikans would not ever change. Their axons and ganglia were tied in knots too intricate to be unraveled in a lifetime. There was no undoing them, and in the meantime they might undo you. A single properly timed "God" or "nation" was enough to set them off. The image of a burning flag, caught in a playback loop, encouraged a condition of permanent fury. The inflammatory effect was intentional. Part of the daily business of revolution involved probing the enemy's anger, finding its roots, and nurturing them: "We have come to feed you on images of what enrages you." Intrusion into cherished psychic spaces, defilement of privacy, became a form of cultural sabotage. Liberals (the kind whose commitment went no further than signing petitions against war) proved especially vulnerable to this tactic. For all their knowl- edgeable references to Norman O. Brown and Herbert Marcuse, they weren't willing to give up their last refuge and let the new age come roaring in.

But there were to be no more refuges. The war was everywhere. Now that lecture halls and cocktail parties were combat zones, the concept of polite behavior stood revealed as just one more instance of pig mind control. The university was not "sacred," it was a training camp for corporate killers. The library was a bin of dead letters. The ROTC building established clearly enough who owned the campus. A meeting was called. Voices shouted for hours through the smoke. Committees representing separate factions raged at one another, as charges of adventurism and coop- tation slammed back and forth. Finally a bearded young man from central casting grabbed the bullhorn and cut through the debate: "While we sit here talking the war is still going on! The killing is still going on, and this university is participating in the killing! The only thing we should be concerned about is whether we're going to sit around on our asses and watch them do it. Because that makes us killers, too! If you're not part of the solution you're part of the problem! I'm asking all of you, are we going to stand for this bullshit?" The ensuing "NO!" was as resounding as could be managed without rehearsal.

They decided to seize the ground, crash through the fences, burn the death factory down if necessary. That was called action. The moment it started, everything became real. Instead of watch- ing a movie they were living one. The bushes and brickwork quivered a bit, as if photographed by a hand-held camera, and the air had the kind of noon blur that Sam Peckinpah liked to capture. Only this time they were the outlaws, they were the Indians. Their armbands glimmered like warpaint. Nothing could stop them, not even the fellow in the loose white cotton shirt, with a copy of the *Bhagavad Gita* tucked under his arm, who tried to intervene outside the cafeteria: "Violence just goes around in circles, man. You're fighting an illusion. Love is the only trip that's real." "You mean we should sit tight and wait for them to put us in the camps? Talk to me in ten years!"

They advanced in spontaneous formation toward the line it was forbidden to cross. The solid world gave way under their feet. With fearful excitement they marched into the heart of transgression. It was as if a wall parted to receive them. They were getting there. They were almost there. Beyond the aperture, history leaned back and waited to be told what to do.

THE PLEASURE
GARDEN

They fucked for hours after the funeral. Their glances had met
as each looked away from the casket, locking into each other's
line of vision and forming for an instant a triangle of which the
third point was the body of their friend. They had sensed all along
that she would finally lead them to this airless vanishing point.
Sitting on the hard pew, Jack kept imagining a door in the air
slamming shut, and almost wanted to leap through it before it
closed, to snatch her back or follow her down that unearthly rabbit
hole. It was springtime again. In the world outside the circle her
death made, France and China and Columbia University were
being taken over by students. People were yelling about Rap
Brown and Clark Gifford and Marshal Giap, *Rat* and *Ramparts*
and *The Wretched of the Earth*, global confrontation and direct
democracy. A war of jargons was in progress. Names were weapons. At that particular moment he wanted nothing more than to
dissolve all the names.

Jack and Jane walked away as fast as they could from the ceremony in the death house. In the solidarity of their retreat they were already becoming lovers. On the way to Jane's little cubbyhole of an apartment in the Village they talked of how their friend had moved toward extinction, with a decisive energy that had made everyone around her feel more alive. During the last few years her pallor and raw edge and occasional madness had made her an icon: the lost girl, the drugged-out waif suicided by the world. It had seemed indispensable for there to be such a person. It was part of the stock melodrama that the time demanded; there was even a subgenre of movies, most of them starring Mimsy Farmer, designed to reenact the same ancient ritual of Death and the Maiden. They had used their friend as a test of reality, a way of telling how close to the borderline they were.

For the moment they just felt very cold. Before long they fell into each other, clung hard to burn the chill away. They felt they were keeping themselves alive. On the turntable the first Beatles album, already nostalgic, repeated over and over. The music created a protected area—a home—but they couldn't quite shake the odor of annihilation they had been sniffing. Each needed to get closer to the other than either of them had ever managed. They burrowed deeper into the hiding place. The bed was a cave where they drilled for fire. They were sounding out the extent of their powers. There were potential worlds inside them. They would become the cave people of a new ice age, hatching languages and mythologies in the dark. They would slam through to the core of themselves and set their bones chiming in archaic Asiatic harmony.

In the morning they again looked at familiar objects and adjusted to the world of flowerpots and bagels and television. The cheerful middle-class pastels of the row houses across the street glistened comfortingly. Over breakfast they watched an old movie, entranced by the courtship rituals of Cary Grant and Irene Dunne. They walked and looked at leaves and squirrels, as if such things had never been seen before; they drank espresso and discussed the aesthetics of the shifting afternoon light; and when it got dark they bought deli sandwiches and cookies and ice cream and went home to their cave. They sealed up the day with lovemaking and decided that henceforth their lives would center on pleasure. Of their old world they would keep the bits that pleased them—Cary Grant or Nova Scotia salmon—and discard the rest. They would be free.

Not that pleasure was simple: the further they entered into it, the more labyrinthine it became. It was all very well to have fun, but which fun? There were the sublime pleasures it hurt to approach, the pleasures that turned souls and bodies inside out; and then there were the deceptive pleasures, the cut-glass pastimes of the bourgeois sitting room, whose function was to stifle the more deep and difficult joys. They had begun a course of instruction, and teachers were everywhere. It was a great time to become lovers; they had lucked upon an age of wonders. The psyche of America had just split open, and rich lodes of marrow were spilling all over the place. An army of experimenters—free-lance scientists bent on recovering ancient kicks—was exploring the byways of mind and nervous system to find where things had gone wrong. The hour had come to undam the main flow. There was to be a resurrection not merely of the five senses but of all the other senses forgotten since the last interglacial epoch.

In thousands of private laboratories—railroad flats, dormitories, endless sprawling lofts—the details of the future world were being fine-tuned. Jack and Jane poked into as many of these secret interiors as they could. They wanted to find out. Sometimes they were awed by the mastery that people had gained over their own lives. In one such space they met a very visible person who announced: "I am a very visual person." The distinction had not yet occurred to them. His purple-and-green tie-dyed shirt and star-spangled bellbottoms were already a landscape. He was a walking hothouse; they could almost see vines sprout from him. His mouth perked sporadically into rascally little grins as he riveted them with his glistening gaze. He might have been a maker of posters or photographs, a patterner of robes, a constructor of magic toys or artfully erotic movies—of artifacts that gratified unstintingly and without apology. Simply to meet him was to become an initiate. He belonged to the race which, having acquired new senses, must find new ways to record sense impressions.

For words he had an offhand contempt: "Language is kind of disgusting, isn't it?" Syntax (he explained) was by now, like any other bureaucratic system, a tangle of exhausted strategies. Henceforth all subordinate clauses ought to be surgically removed, leaving only the most elemental imperatives: Do it now! Further! ZAP! "All the rest of it is just a compound of evasive gestures—the kind of conversation that the uptight people in the compulsively neat living rooms use to disguise their boredom. If you examine it close up, it disintegrates. You ought to see what happens to those people when they take acid and forget how to talk. Their mouths flap like fish out of water. They force out the stillborn phrases—'Why are we—' 'If only—' 'What is it going to—' 'Can't you see?'— and they end up weeping, falling to pieces altogether, just because their neat travel-book expressions disappear on them. You know: See It and Say It in Language. They try to crawl into the rug, into the air of the room, to find out which way the words went. I have seen this. They want to chase the words. Like little children, they think the words have *gone* somewhere, and if you tell them the words were never there to begin with they start weeping again. They sit there, those grown-up children, helplessly overeducated, suddenly all alone with their eyes. The world comes rushing in and scares the hell out of them. They never noticed it before. They are verbal people, they have been living a half-life of secondhand meanings. You know: Everything happened a long time ago and it's written down in a book.''

That cyclonic rush—the honing of existence down to a pure and relentless present tense—was precisely what the very visual person *liked* about the world. It fed him wherever he stumbled on it: in the effects of certain drugs, in certain examples of advertising art, in sudden upsurges of the sexy or the grotesque or the outrageously campy, in anything that permitted him to be taken over by raw perception. He related all this to Jack and Jane with an almost jaded air that somehow induced confidence. In his loft he had made a dwelling where pleasure came pouring in at the eyes. Within his gates the world consisted of unexpected chunks of neon and acrylic and celluloid, alcoves that glimmered and became lagoons, hallways that narrowed into erotically rounded portholes, mysterious hidden bedrooms that redefined the body. It was a space to get lost in. The self-generating figurations flowed continuously outward. The verticals blinked and commenced their in-and-out, in-and-out. The undulating polka dots swept the whole visual field into their choreography. Names died in that swirl. All of this (the very visual person explained) was designed so that he could relax and enjoy what was being done to his nervous system. It was like waking up: with big mindless eyes he wallowed in texture and contour and crazy shadows that reversed themselves and became a sort of wet light. This was the beginning of the language in which the history of the future would be written. Ultimately, he confided, we would all share a living alphabet of wavy lines curving inward, like the spiral shape Dr. Wilhelm Reich had proposed as an ideogrammic representation of orgasm.

For a long time after they left that party they thought about what he had said, especially the last bit. Everything always came back to orgasm, which had become the universally appropriate metaphor and formal model. The lovers in bed could rightly feel that they were at the center of the age. It was as if the culture had determined to mirror their passion. The guitar solo started slow and low and built to an almost unbearably loud and palpitant climax. The light show's detonating blobs of color surged toward a blinding brightness that erased the world. Sexual orgasm was the Rosetta Stone through which one could tune in to an infinite range of analogous phenomena: visual orgasms, aural orgasms, aromatic orgasms, even philosophical orgasms. All meaningful form could be summarized as foreplay crescendoing toward peak and release. All zones were erogenous. In each of its nooks and seams and strata, the human organism was chiefly designed for explosions of pleasure. All that was necessary was to stop resisting.

The ultimate goal, as Jane remarked one day, was the total resensualizing of the world. It was not a question of having sex at every instant but of perceiving each instant as sexual. To breathe was an erotic act. The universe was nothing but an extrapolation of sexual energy. The very rocks quivered in their beds of earth. The ocean's nerve endings manifested themselves in the form of translucent wavering vegetation. The planet inhaled and exhaled in accordance with cyclical ripples of pleasure. Within that macrocosmic breathing, an orgasm was no isolated event. It was a feeling out of invisible structural lines, a tuning in to celestial harmonics. By surrendering to sheer gratification, the nervous system came into contact with the latent architecture of what could only be called the Godhead. The most intimate shoots of sensation hooked up directly with the force binding atom to atom and galaxy to galaxy. That was why an orgasm seemed to turn the world inside out. Seeing the real face of matter for the first time, the lovers stared at each other in amazement: "So *that's* what we're made of."

There had not always been such a surfeit of colors and pleasures.

This thing had only just kicked on. Jack and Jane felt privileged to be in on the start of a new epoch, a turn in human history as decisive as the advent of the Neolithic. They were witnessing the onset of a transition from darkness into light. The race was at last preparing to abandon its primeval cult of suffering and initiate the millennium of joy. Lying in bed in the calm darkening afternoon, they reminisced about the drab old days whose texture now seemed so remote. Remember when the world was flat, and the cars moved unconsciously through cluttered blight, and people conceived of their bodies as some sort of ponderous luggage? The landscape back then consisted of overlapping street signs reflecting layers of glare. The pedestrians had no sense of spatial depth: no sense, indeed, that the street as such actually existed. No one then could have conceived, for instance, of Sun Ra's message: "Space Is the Place." It was as if the storefronts were yanked along on pulleys, and the people of the city vacantly watched them pass. The baked sluggish towns of their childhood receded into gas stench and numb highway lines. That was in 1948, or 1956, or 1960. The bridge was buried in wires. The way to work was demarcated by window holes and rectangular blocks containing words. There was a lumpish head to which lotion was applied. Money was distributed from little slits cut from black-and-white warehouses. The citizens began to feel there was no longer anything to look at. The world was so familiar that their senses had atrophied. With toylike awkwardness they bent their ears toward the first noisy traces of air conditioning. But in this world even noises made no noise, and the most abrasive pinks seemed oddly quiescent. The days merely passed. In the corners of bus depots fuzzy shadows piled up. The closets of freshly swept homes were haunted by nothing more monstrous than the ghosts of Brillo pads—and that innocuousness was in itself monstrous.

In this vacuum the only intrusions came from accidental violence or unanticipated decay. The grating as it lost its paint offered a small explosion of hidden green streaks. A bag of vegetables flattened by a truck embellished an otherwise colorless turnpike. These were extravagances, things not meant to be there. And what, in the midst of all those inert and bulky objects, could have been more extravagant than the body, with its outrageous insistence on transforming the world into a replica of its desires? It wanted green and it would have it. It wanted the body of the beloved and would if necessary tear down all walls to get to it. So their revolution began in nakedness, in the restitution of Eden. "We were born naked, and that's how we want to stay." They intended to divest themselves of everything: clothes, furniture, cities, grammars, armies.

In the new world there would be no more walls. The harsh deformed churches and states would be dissolved by the force of the desires they had attempted to contain. The Piscean culture could not generate, only thwart. The ancestral impulse to repress had petrified into a dead landscape of prisons and brothels and army camps. The children had grown up in the boxlike preserves whose fake shrubbery and studio backdrops concealed the real setup. It had taken them years to learn what their own half-strangled sexual responses had been trying to teach them: that every city plan was a diagram of how to prevent the body from asserting its natural laws. The Council of Elders had bequeathed a society that resembled a chastity belt or instrument of bondage. But now the crisis had come. The daemon of sexuality welled up from within to burst the forms that enclosed it.

Lovers needed no battle cry beyond their own bodies. They participated in the revolution by making love. Every freely and lovingly offered blow job, for instance, was a blow against empire. Their casual nakedness short-circuited the enforced morality by which the police state and its ally, organized religion, conspired to make a fetish of voyeurism and prostitution. Sexual freedom was the paradigm of every other freedom. The surrender to desire, the embrace, the unshackled amorous cries: these were the authentic cataclysms of which wars and civil rituals and political upheavals were but feeble parodies. If humans could reconcile themselves to a sensual vegetable life, the killing would stop. Having once experienced that unburdening, who would want to kill? Who would be so absurd? Perhaps the elders had always dreaded that: the moment when the young would so give way to the delights of their own bodies that they would neither fight the old men's wars nor submit to be harnessed for their slave labor. What if they gave a war and everybody was too busy making out in the underbrush to care?

Jack and Jane sensed that the world outside the window was a hostile formation, a codified insult to the infinite tenderness they were beginning to chart. They were themselves the edge. The human universe was bounded by the bedframe. A single caress recapitulated millennia of ancestral experience. It was all inside them, the struggle of life against death, of pity against cruelty. Now it was up to them to change the way they touched or responded to a touch. What other starting point could there be? The old reflexes were to be unlearned one by one. There were even schools for that process, California institutes of higher unlearning. But there was no need to go so far afield. They could make of their life together their own private Esalen. They would study to divest themselves of an unwanted legacy of neural jams and bottlenecks. They came across the phrase "somatic awareness" and began to realize what that might mean, what meadowlike flows of feeling might be attainable. They talked about how nice it would be to live without words. It was time for the hairsplitting manias of the alienated brain—Thomas Aquinas and his five thousand vacuum-packed intellectual categories—to melt into a caressing sea of patchouli oil.

The hot weather came and they were ready for it. They sought out a suburban hideaway, house-sitting for friends of friends so they could borrow some air and space, hang out naked by the pool, and listen to surf music all morning. Of a fenced-in patio on Locust Drive they made their California. Surf music was the ideal sound track, the anthem of the body, a butter-smooth harmony wider and deeper than thought, and empty enough to contain sun and sky and ocean: "Catch a wave and you're sitting on top of the world." The light by the water let them let go. In the great book of the flesh, shrubbery and genitalia and falsetto chants were bound together into an iridescent continuum. A sparrow flickered in a corner of the lawn as the breeze swept across the sundeck. The imagination of a wave possessed them. The cosmos flexed itself in a great pelvic lurch just as the Beach Boys surged toward the finale of "Don't Back Down."

They aspired toward the torpor of the cat stretching languorously under the coffee table. In the heat they donned Ray-Bans and assisted at the dissolution of history. That this weekend paradise was not really theirs—that its trappings were as lavishly unreal as a movie set—made it all the more seamlessly pleasant. It was titillating to trespass on such luxury. The half-parted glass door and cedarwood paneling, the sofas and carpets and enormous beds would have made perfect props for a soap opera in Metrocolor, in which Lana Turner in furs would glide toward murder or adultery, stalked by voluptuous camera movements. The furniture had been paid for with anxiety. But Jack and Jane had for the moment found a way to beat the system. They got the upholstery without the guilt.

At night they dimmed the lights of their palace to smoke marijuana and watch horror movies. Some channel was always showing *Psychomania* or *Dementia 13* or *The Horror Chamber of Doctor Faustus*, intercut with clips of a thinly mustached man talking about New Jersey real estate. The scratchy footage of this man—

pacing land lots carved out of heavily wooded areas, or stealthily opening the doors of white, isolated houses—could easily have come from one of the horror movies. The land salesman had the same abrasive and inexpressive delivery as the post-synched stranglers and mad doctors. The ads and the movies combined to evoke a late-night geography of fear and alienation. None of it frightened them anymore. So pleased were they to discover this that they gorged on the images. What most delighted them was a particular blend of lust, resentment, and absolute fakeness. The movies functioned like an emotional striptease, ripping away layers of nuance and sensitivity to reach a core where Luana Anders or Gloria Talbott raged woodenly. The comic-book crudeness of the characters and the unmodulated tonelessness of the acting brought the movies closer to the real. It was the subtlety of "genuine" actors—the Oliviers and Bancrofts and Dewhursts—that was suspect. High culture served as an elaborate device for masking perception of what the C-movies wallowed in.

The movies showed them the country they had been born into: a shadowland of perverse figurines. Their brains, they were discovering, consisted of images of blondes in cocktail lounges, masked men climbing through suburban windows, frightened helpless housewives, cop cars blocking off exits. They inhabited a neural landscape symbolically represented by various forms of seduction and restraint. A tight strapless gown or a trenchcoat was not a garment, it was a state of being. The existentialists had been onto something all along: sexy clothes preceded essence. You stepped into the available wardrobe and became authentic. It was impossible even to imagine nakedness, since the word already implied the existence of clothing, of concealment. They looked at each other's faces and wondered at what masks they were. How strange it was to be "Jack" or "Jane" and to have these predictable motivations planted in them, as if they had been constructed by a tired scenarist already numb from having written *Teen-age Crime Wave* or *Tormented*.

They had come to the movies to laugh and be aroused, but they stayed for more perplexing reasons. In the washed-out faces flitting across the screen they hoped perhaps to find again the face they had lost: the face of their dead friend. The afterimage of that face was still strong enough for them to toy with the notion of somehow dragging it into the world, instead of letting it fade and die its second, final death. Film was precisely the kind of marshy country where phantoms might linger. Many of the movies—the ones that most captivated them played on this temptation to reanimate. They were haunted by the resurrection of dead women, the Islamic vampire in *Beast of Morocco* or Barbara Steele's disfigured witch in *Black Sunday*. The caves and concealed tombs where those alluring and malevolent spirits lay in wait were like the back rooms of Jack's mind and Jane's mind. Sometimes at night, in the space between them in the dark, they sensed a third presence. In the movies the catalyst for breaking down the barrier between being and nonbeing was always some kind of forbidden sex magic. They imagined something similar happening to them, as if the heat of their loins generated not a child but a ghost.

Autumn nagged at them like a personal loss. They wanted the sun to halt in its tracks, to keep the pool warm for them. The approaching cold hinted at a descent into a blackness they would have preferred not to confront. It was also the season of registering for academic courses and, in Jack's case, of attempting to maintain an already problematic draft status. They conceived of their life in the outer world chiefly as a shoring up of defenses through the manipulation of forms, cards, dossiers. As long as the appropriate code numbers were cross-indexed against your name, you were free to go on living your real life a little longer. They bought breathing space with the fulfillment of minimum requirements.

Somehow they managed to shuffle ahead, although "ahead" was not where they felt like going. The path that attracted them was curved, lateral, inward. There was something to be entered: an aperture like the cave Ali Baba found. They hacked at underbrush, looking for a hidden gate.

Jane found the way in. She showed up one afternoon with two purple tablets so immaculate that they had to be the purest possible acid, the handiwork not of Mafia bootleggers but of the legendary, already vanishing generation of underground chemical saints. Jack held one of the tablets in his hand and studied its tint and shape and texture. It was such a discrete and palpable thing, a hard little pebble alone in the universe. Something about it made him shiver. Here was not merely the world in a grain of sand, but all the worlds and antiworlds in a bit of compacted powder. The palm of his hand had never seemed more immense.

They saved it for nighttime, decking the room in bright patterned fabrics and laying out in advance what they hoped would be a suitable soundtrack: Miles Davis and Ravi Shankar and some Bach harpsichord music. They knelt together on a cushion, attempting to reconstruct intuitively some rite of exorcism or initiation salvaged from Delphi or Akkad or Mohenjo-Daro. As they swallowed the tablets they stared into each other's eyes. It was solemn and exciting. They would hold hands and disappear together into another world. After a while their teeth began to ache, and their tongues tasted of blood as if they had been running. The Miles Davis had been playing for a very long time. Had there ever been a time when it had not been playing? They could just barely recall such a time, a remote archaeological epoch when they also had names and had been sitting in something called an apartment. It had been 1968 and for some reason they had decided to swallow a sort of tablet.

Without moving they had crossed the dividing line. Here was

that other world: and it turned out, of course, to be the only real one, the lost one. For a moment Jack had a panicked sense that he was going blind, only to realize that he had been gripped by a fear of seeing. There was a painful surge (the pain came from resistance) as the new powers of sight and hearing broke through. Gradually the pain dissolved into knowledge. These were the powers they had been born with, their original senses restored at last. Their fingertips had become frighteningly sensitive. To accidentally brush against corduroy was to find among its ridges a microcosmic mountain range: "Look, it's the Himalayas." This was where the real spaces had been hidden all along. They remembered the rooms within rooms, the intergalactic tundras secreted in the gaps between household objects. They looked at each other and saw that each was as big as a planet: huge god bodies perched on absurdly dinky furniture. Their mouths were vast. They got lost in miles of complicated teeth, labyrinths of tongue tissue. Their slightest whisper thundered. There was a noise like a factory, which turned out to be the roar of their blood.

Somehow they were going to crawl through this jungle of sense impressions and make a clearing and make love. That was why they had come here in the first place. After all, sex on acid—or what Timothy Leary had once called "an ultimate merging with a person of the opposite sex"—was the newest and therefore the most powerful of erotic fantasies, the secret promise underlying the swirl of psychedelic props and lighting effects. What were the flickers and fabrics and streaks of body paint for, if not to magnify the central ecstasy? All the accoutrements of the new world converged on a genital axis, a bridal chamber surrounded by paisley curtains.

Their path to that chamber became a process of finding openings within openings within openings. The retina was the first point of entry. Their eyes, which had been floundering unfocused among the waves of textures, met across space. Their crisscrossed gazes clicked into position. They had found the link. Each would journey toward the source of the other's glance. The distance between them—an infinite expanse of some two or three feet—hung suspended like a visible anguish. They felt they had to cut away at the air that separated them. Each saw the light in the other's eye out there and wanted it to be here, inside. But they experienced their movement toward each other as a series of microscopically detailed freeze-frames. What the images registered was not "things" but splash marks, momentary traces of an underlying eddying force. They surrendered to the rhythm of a lovemaking that had nothing to do with willed action, an unfolding that carried them passively along. It was slower than anything they had ever imagined. There was a period of several centuries during which their eyelashes brushed against each other. Nothing could be hurried. The caresses in which they found themselves immersed were a massaging away of mysterious barriers. They came closer and closer together through a kind of erosion.

Many thousands of years would go by before they were permitted to rediscover their private parts. They descended into their own bodies like hominids foraging in new territory, alert to every vein and grotto they encountered. Meanwhile—as if in another life—their minds were assaulted by grotesque love scenes, obscene parodies of old movies, reenactments of chaotic playground games from before the age of speech. To burrow beyond the image track they had to pass through multiple rapes, tortures, punishments. Robed executioners flickered into visibility before melting back into the bedframe's screws or the window gate's grillwork. With each caress they were peeling away layers of history and language. This kind of excavation had no end. The more they emptied themselves of themselves, the more there was to be experienced. They swam in a raw world: a gluey collage of fur and bone where there was no north or south, no up or down.

The millennia it had taken to bring them to the point of actually fucking had been a necessary preparation for what might otherwise have terrified them. They had not realized just how peculiar it would seem to be incarnate in these bodies. Until this moment they had always been in some sense voyeurs at their own love-making. The place where sex happened had remained *other*: a well or submerged ocean existing *beneath* them, or a creature they surmounted and allowed on occasion to transport them. They used it to pleasure themselves, as they used wine or marijuana. But on this night everything had been turned inside out. They were being taught that they did not in any sense *have* private parts, that they as so-called individual personalities were merely the public parts of a body they had never even dared to imagine. What a realm they had entered: the true underworld, the nether region asserting its primacy in nether language. The landscape formed by the conjunction of their bodies might have been the surface of Venus, its clefts and basins visible at last from beneath the planet's cloud cover. The joy that circulated among its channels was fierce, almost inhuman. The "human"—that condition of ordinary numbness—they had discarded like a snakeskin.

From that plateau of unfamiliarity they gradually subsided, and in the process separated out into selves. Ecstasy would take some getting used to. They could not have remained much longer among such peculiar flora. Wandering randomly about the apartment, they found themselves imitating the gestures of domesticity. They clicked lights on or off, shook out blankets, tidied. The chairs they sat in restored a sense of bodily structure, reminding them where the neck was, where the spine, where the buttocks. They drank water from cups, and marveled at how skillfully they did so. They smoked, and the world grew flat. As the light leaked in from the street, they were quietly pleased to be among clocks and shoes. During this process of reentry Jack leafed idly through a copy of *TV Guide*. However comical and baroque it seemed—a

155

timetable swollen with melodramas, fetishes, and pictures of food—he also found it unexpectedly soothing. He grew almost tearful at the glimpses of families in campers, of couples sharing a seaside cigarette. It was a message from his far-off native land.

After a tomblike sleep they woke to find themselves Jack and Jane once more. It was already late afternoon. Jane looked at her hand: it was just a hand. They felt it was important to start talking about what had happened, but it took them a while to find a way. New terms had to be invented to describe where they had been, and the things that had transpired there. "Did you have that wavering sensation with your body, I mean sort of like a waterfall but more solid, made of rubbery silk maybe?" "I knew what the fire dots were doing, they were laying themselves out in like an alphabet and I understood it." "The air was made of layers of translucent curtains and they would kind of shift. Every time they shifted my eyes went deeper into what was there." "I suddenly thought: After all this time I finally understand what *inside* means. It's nothing like anybody said."

Obviously what they had experienced should be kept alive. However, they soon started slipping backward. It was extremely difficult even to remember what had taken place that night. To describe it was to lose it. The mechanisms of language and memory were not designed to cope with such phenomena—in fact, they were designed to obliterate them. Ordinary consciousness survived by erasing whatever perceptions did not fit its pigeonholes. Jack and Jane were thus conspiring to circumvent the brain's filing system. It turned out to be a little like trying to sneak up behind yourself. Finally they developed a theory that what they were trying to remember could by its nature not be remembered. Nostalgia was forbidden. If it wasn't happening, it was as if it had never happened. It could only be experienced. That was what made it special.

Jane knew a guy, a grad student, who had originally been a physics major but was now engaged in systematically comparing the imagery employed by the sixteenth-century mystic St. John of the Cross with that of certain Amazonian *curanderos*. They ran into him one afternoon and ended up having a long conversation about shamanism, healing rituals, and the identity of the mysterious drug *soma* that was worshipped as a god in ancient India. A few weeks later he invited them to a party, and Jane seemed to feel that it would be an important event. "He and his friends are always dropping little hints about peyote and psilocybin and things like that." There must have been fifty or sixty people at the party when they showed up. Everybody was handed a pristine white capsule at the door. The apartment consisted of a series of long narrow rooms, each lined with cushions and draped in fabric of luxurious brilliance. People drifted according to temperament into the green room or the turquoise room or the purple room. There was none of the usual party chatter, only a low steady-state hum, the sound of a beehive. It wasn't easy to make out what people were saying, because in every room a speaker at ceiling level piped in music from an unseen source. It was a record by a group called Iron Butterfly. It was loud and reverberant, and soon as it ended, it began again. The capsules contained a very pure grade of mescaline. The guests (there were nearly a hundred by now) for the most part waited quietly for the drug to take effect.

Jane leaned over and whispered to Jack, "Before it gets too crazy I want to take care of something. Wait for me." He had stayed close to her, as if to form a world apart from the rest of the room. Her disappearance nudged him into what was going on. People sat cross-legged on the cushions, looking at each other across a narrow divide, communicating with facial expressions. The music, because of the way it annihilated conversation, became a kind of hush. The faces isolated against the white plaster backdrop reminded Jack of an Italian movie he had seen called *The Gospel According to St. Matthew*. In fact, the situation began to seem decidedly biblical. They sat in rows like the guests at the feast of Pentecost, and their eyes beamed out messages which—if he was reading this glistening lingo correctly—indicated that the Dove was actually about to descend, right above their heads, roughly on a level with the speakers. The barbaric resonance of the Iron Butterfly was the harbinger of an electrochemical baptism. The guitars were helping to crack the sky open. The Holy Spirit would come rushing in through the jagged gaps the reverb made. "We're all in the room together," Jack thought, or said: the distinction had become immaterial. They were sitting inside their minds and their minds had meanwhile spilled out into a common pool. They were souls gathered in a steam bath in the New Jerusalem. The shape of the air between their faces was their collective face. It was shaped like a cup. It gave off light. They smiled as they leaned forward to drink from its radiance.

Jane materialized from the dark hallway. As he caught her eye she winked with secretive satisfaction. The instant she appeared Jack realized he had been close to panic. The sense of bathing had been about to give way to a sense of drowning. All his senses had been on guard against an encroaching absorption. "Do you mind if we get out of here?" he said with restrained urgency. "But I thought you wanted to see what it was like." "If it's all right I'd rather be alone with you. I think we can just make it downtown before we lose control, okay?" "Okay." By now their legs were barely functioning, but they managed to somehow roll down into the chilled street. They moved like overgrown plants escaped from a greenhouse. Clinging to vestiges of human speech and gesture, they succeeded in hailing a taxi and giving instructions to its driver, in phrases that resembled translations from some Balkan dialect. They clutched keys and money in their hands, terrified that their brains would dissolve before they had gotten through the door beyond which everything was permitted.

As the knob turned and the door swung inward into their own dark space, they felt like comic book characters finally free (in the absence of witnesses) to transform their bodies. By the time they reached the other side they were loose clusters of flame. Clothes and language fell from them. The rug toward which they slid was phosphorescent soil. Their bodies soaked up its greenish bluish glow. In that night garden, in an air heavy with herbs and fluids, they reinvented the Old Religion, the pre-Christian nature cult of the witches. It was for this they had split off from the main group: to sink into a private ritual, a magic whose boundaries they would determine for themselves, without guides or gurus. They held the power in their hands: literally, as it turned out. When Jack, toward dawn, asked Jane where she had gone off to at the party, she reached into her purse and extracted a wad of Saran wrap. As she unrolled it, twenty-four white capsules tumbled out to form an impromptu relief map, a prospect of mountains stretching toward an unimaginable future.

Their course of self-education (for so they defined it from the start) soon fell into a regular cadence. The drug was the text, the rest of their lives a commentary on it. This was a book written in flesh and blood, which they read by swallowing. Each chapter took them deeper, introduced new levels of vocabulary. They were getting more accomplished by the month, strong enough to understand more and more of the instructions of the little god walled up within the capsule. The hardest test came on New Year's Eve. They had refused all invitations, taken the phone off the hook, and prepared themselves for a rite of transition. By the time the next year dawned—the year that would complete this most extraordinary of decades—they would be new people. Nothing less was demanded of them. Their ego selves would shrivel in the first light like a vampire. But it went on much longer than expected. The drug didn't want to let go. There was a further hell they were obliged to pass through, a domain of infantile thirsts and preprogramed gag responses, of night terrors and suffocation by weeping. They learned they were vessels in which tears had been imprisoned. The technique of not crying—mastered at an early age— had provided a structural model for subsequent personality development. Their social selves had crystallized around a withheld teardrop that was now to be liberated. But once the waters started pouring it was hard to stop them. If they let them all flow out, what would be left? "Jack" and "Jane" would simply evaporate. It was like shrinking to the dimensions of a baby's soft-boned body and sobbing in a dark that might never end. They had not sought to be reminded of what an overwhelming and terrifying place the body had once been. But having stranded themselves in this jungle, having become Hansel and Gretel once more, they had to find an exit.

"If we could only cut loose from these damn coils." They stumbled along twisting swamp trails. Nothing was clear. Nothing was straight. They had spilled beyond their limits. In their place a mess of molecules slopped haphazardly about the room. Bits would cohere. A perfect tongue formed, but it didn't know where it ended. A childhood bedtime experience took place in their midst, but it couldn't quite figure out whose childhood it was part of. The whole body became momentarily perceptible, but it was nearly dead: a marble sarcophagus lid complete with veins and tendons. The vital movements had been unaccountably abandoned on the other side of a particular inhalation. The breath would have to be pulled out to get it back. But that would mean peeling the lungs away like a coat. What if, in all this confusion, one of them were to accidentally discard something essential? They were wondering about what held them together inside, what held the world together, what kept them in the world or would take them out of it, what manner of hole they would be sucked through at last. "It's all on a thread, we're like accidents."

Jack clicked the light on and grabbed a book. It could have been any book. He craved words, definite arrangements of meanings, the authority of a declarative statement terminating in a period. A book was a dry shore offering rescue from the world ocean. To open the book was to clamber up on a solid shelf. But as he opened this one—it was *The Murder of Christ* by Wilhelm Reich, the one the multimedia artist had recommended but which neither had until now so much as glanced at—he was plunged into fresh waters by a single phrase: "the streaming sensation." The streaming sensation, he read, was held back by armor. The armor was the shape of a personality, a pattern of muscular tension forming a barricade against the world and against any other living being. From behind the barricade the flow fought to get out. Jack realized he was reading an exact description of what had been going on in the room. Seeing his own truth written down by another hand was like the apparition of a ghost. The letters wriggled against the page's blinding white. Each *s* coiled in serpentine confirmation of the bioenergetic current Reich was attempting to describe.

Jack split in two. Half of him was still in the room. The other half began to enter a coherent world made out of words such as "vegetative" and "plasmatic" and "pulsation." It was the world of Reich's thought, or more properly it was Reich himself, alive in the syntactic web that pulsed and flowed in sympathy with— no, identical with—that streaming sensation about which it was talking. Jack didn't want the book to lead away from the room, he wanted to channel it into the room. "You'll never believe what's going on in this book, it explains everything we've been feeling." He began to read it aloud, his breathing harmonizing with the assertive power of the sentences. The voice in his throat was not his. A wise ancestor used him as a vessel to bring this message into the world. His voice swelled until he couldn't carry it anymore. So that, he thought, is what it's like to be a prophet.

The night went on for days. Things got stickier and stickier. There was too much clutter. They wanted to be loose and clear and straight with each other, they wanted to get right with the spirit, but details kept getting in the way. When they finally started to calm down, after some thirty hours of the barrage, they felt like exhausted veterans. They remembered, for example, how strange it had been to walk through the city not remembering what money was. They had forced themselves outside because they needed sustenance. They had felt themselves dying: "We have to have juice." The sick fluorescence of the supermarket drew them toward the automatic doors, past which the life-giving orange liquid was stored in waxy paper containers. They would not soon forget their passage through the check-out lane, their painful struggle to handle the green paper correctly. "We just wanted to drink some orange juice, that's all," Jack attempted to explain to the clerk. Each such foray was an obstacle course. So much had to be memorized to avoid inappropriate gestures. Only when they were alone together could they feel free. They shared the beginnings of a common language. One of them could look at the room and say, "This rug is a trap," or "There have to be more openings here," and expect to be understood.

They were learning to stand outside their old selves, the selves they were shedding. It was a kind of athletic training. They could go for longer and longer periods without having to resort to stock characterizations. Their new selves were smooth, flexible, glistening with vitality. It was great when they felt themselves really being like that. It gave them the incentive to keep discarding the accumulated junk of their psyches, tuning themselves up to a state of constant awareness. If they could only get through this winter of bewilderment, they might be ready for satori by springtime.

The trick was to cut through the tangles left over from the past: not just their immediate past, but the former lives whose residue began to extrude from the cracks in their current existence. Sometimes, in the dark especially, they caught disturbing glimpses of people they had been. At moments the room filled with a swarming chorus of unseen beings. Faint tunes and whispered fragments of poems or scriptures announced the presence of these emissaries. "You approached the casement. The tower was in the light. I was in the spiral winding on the shadowed side." The whispers nibbled at the room's solidity; the bed seemed suspended in midair, and Jack and Jane had a sense of being watched from another plane. There were layers upon layers of reality, an infinite series of frequencies of which the "Jack and Jane world" represented one random channel. It was quite possible that the room really was full of conscious disembodied minds tuning in to an adjacent band width. Unusual spinal activity might serve as a signaling device.

Some of these phenomena were unquestionably eerie. An almost inaudible hissing, for instance, shaped itself into words; it could easily be taken for "the voice of the tempter." Plaintive voices called from a great distance—thousands of years of distance—as if to say, "When are you coming over here?" At times it felt like being jerked around by invisible instructors. The onset of these occurrences was always the same. It happened when they looked into each other's eyes. They would get lost for hours. They fell down a well together, just like Alice or the astronaut in *2001*. There might be a dot they were moving toward, a focal pinpoint. It would swell and swallow them and then they would be *in* it: except they were no longer "they" and there was nothing at all to hold on to. This engulfment either felt good or it didn't. When it felt good was almost the scariest, because they became actual gods.

They could almost remember the time before they made the world. They even came close to restoring it. They rode on clouds. The translucent sky palace that was their real home became manifest for as long as they could avoid conceptualizing it. Thought killed the divine. Lovemaking, however, killed thought, and in the process reawakened latent deities. By turns they were Jove and Juno, Krishna and Radha, Izanami and Izanagi, pharaonic siblings consummating a sacred marriage. The old mythologies welcomed them with reminders of what they had once been and could still become. They fled toward a polytheistic wilderness sparkling with god-blossoms, god-trees, god-stones.

It would only be necessary to kill whatever ghost of Christianity still lingered in them. They came to this conclusion while leafing through a history of art. Each color plate was a world to be tried out. They could be Chinese or Ceylonese or Maori: anything but descendants of the European Christians whose death cult had jinxed them in the womb. The God of the Last Judgment stared out vacant as a skull, while sinners tumbled toward an excremental hell. "Let's skip this page, I want to get back to the Persian garden."

Asia had the specific answers to most of their questions, questions the West had not even had the sense to ask. They immersed themselves in vigorous calligraphic ink splashes, in the fleshlike wriggling and curling of Chinese mountain ranges, in the bare clean silence of a Zen pond. They memorized Sanskrit love manuals and amorous odes: "She stumbles bewitchingly as she moves, revealing her whirlpool-navel." In the intertwining bodies of the Konarak temple carvings they found sustenance for their own erotic energies. Loose robes and lightweight sandals liberated them from the bondage of Western clothing. Japanese lanterns and reproductions of scroll paintings transformed the walls. With long-playing tapes of oud and veena and shakuhachi they distended their notion of time, discovering fresh repositories of duration among the microtones.

In Oriental art nothing was accidental. Every hallucinatory effect had been planned in advance by conspiratorial brush masters. It was like being winked at across an abyss. But not all hidden messages came from the East. They were finding them all over the place now, tiny hints deposited by a secret primeval community of initiates. Throughout history these agents had been guarding the core of wisdom. Even in the shadow of Catholic inquisitors and Calvinist thought police they had nurtured the doctrine of eternal subversion: that reality is divine and wonderfully pointless play. As Gnostics, the agents had described a mandalalike cosmos of aeons within aeons emanating from an infinite center. As Taoists, they had roamed the hills of China drinking wine and writing ecstatic poems. As Persian miniaturists, they had recorded the textures of a landscape whose blue-and-pink soil rippled with bioenergetic impulses. They could turn up anywhere. Most recently they had surfaced as jazz musicians with names like Sun Ra and Pharoah Sanders, playing an African music of gongs and drums and wails for hours on end, loud enough to wake the dead. The living spirit, secreted in an Egyptian pyramid, was bursting out from its sepulcher amid shrieks and trumpetings.

The musicians wore robes and demarcated their performance space with strategic ankhs and lotuses. The music seemed to provide a channel for the ancient ones. Jack and Jane started to think that they, too, could be conduits. The only limits were self-created. When they overheard what was really going on in *Karma* and *Tauhid* and *Jewels of Thought* they laughed almost as uncontrollably as they had once wept. It was a bubbling laughter, the voice of a belly spirit, a free immortal god who had taken up temporary residence inside them. "Listen, they're playing their *thing*!" Jack or Jane exclaimed with perfect lucidity. Leon Thomas initiated a peristaltic chant, spontaneous, self-regulating, potentially endless. He wasn't "doing" anything, he was allowing something to come out. The vibration that made use of his lungs and vocal cords didn't belong to anybody. It circulated: "The wind bloweth where it listeth." It blew through the trumpets and saxophones and set the drums clattering in its wake. It was the noise of spirit storming into the world.

Jack and Jane tried it on their own. Their first OM was rather forced, a line read by an amateur actor. They had to learn to stop saying it and let it say them. The vowel sound was permanently open; the consonant was permanently shut. To sound them simultaneously was to realize the unity behind all duality. The seed syllable embodied the mystery of form. It wasn't just a word. In some sense it was, literally, the creator. First came the sound. Then the body was made, as a means for carrying the sound. But the source of the sound was inside them, bound in an infinitely small space that contained infinity. This was not allegory or metaphor. It was there. It was there in their bodies. It made the world.

But what a world it had made, a world of horrors. Murderous pellets barked against the walls, obscene challenges violated boundary lines, canisters demolished protective screens. Just beyond the window, the culture of gasoline was seeping toward the fire that would explode it. All the supply lines and intersections were armored. Radar equipment designated coordinates for remote-control killing. Bodies were regularly burned, smashed, mutilated. The textures they were discovering in their room, in themselves, could barely survive outside those four walls. As it was, he might be dragged from the room. At any moment a draft notice requisitioning his body might arrive. He had been trying to forget about it, but the thought had a way of intruding in the middle of the night. He would cling to her then as if armed men were about to barge in and pry him from her. Sometimes they seemed to be crawling inside each other. If they got far enough in they would find the safe soft place.

For Jack that place was the domain of Woman: the reverse side of history, the realm of the unmanifested. The secret of the present era was a magic to which Jane had primary access. She was the teacher, leading him into the same depths that the old mystery religions had explored. It was solely through her grace that a series of miracles began to occur, and it was she who afterward explained what had happened. "Do you realize there are names for all these experiences? The sense we had of everything mixing is called synesthesia. It's like in the Leon Thomas song when he talks about 'where echoes shine and reflections ring.' That's how babies perceive things until they learn to organize their sensory input. Neat, isn't it?"

They had figured out that by snorting the mescaline rather than swallowing it they could achieve a blindingly swift entry into the other world. The first time they tried it he was staring at her, and in a matter of seconds she metamorphosed into a sort of dark goddess, an apparition forming out of nothing like the genie released from the bottle in *The Thief of Bagdad*. He had an irresistible impulse to kneel and worship. He opened his mouth as if to speak, but what emerged was unlike anything he had ever heard. A tremulous growl poured out of its own volition. An impossibly deep and craggy voice spoke a language beyond transcription. It moved up through him using his lungs and larynx in an altogether unfamiliar but profoundly knowing way. It knew what to do with him. It spoke of that and of much else: the making of the ocean, the distances between the stars, the alchemical formulas locked up in matter. Its speech was like the sound of foam. It kept coming out because what it had to say went on forever. It only ended when he became aware of Jane rubbing his shoulders and whispering somewhat anxiously, "Maybe it's time to stop now, huh?" He tried his voice again and this time it was him, sounding tiny and creaky by comparison. Once again Jane knew what was going on. "That's called glossolalia. I've read about it, but I never actually heard it before. It sounded pretty authentic."

Around this time they began to worry more than before. They had marched into the country of the spirits, and now the spirits were peeping out from behind the bushes. In their dreams bright mask faces admonished them to watch their step. They felt increasingly like trespassers. There was a barrier that kept them from fully entering the world they had been spying on all these months. It was a divide as thin as thread but strong as iron. Something fundamental remained to be broken down. It had to do with death. "Maybe we only die because we cling to life. If we were willing to die we might live forever, our consciousness, I mean. Don't you feel that?" But they weren't quite sure that they did feel that, or wanted to feel that. They couldn't decide if the immortality of the soul was a threat or a promise.

They had kept going on until they reached the tip of the tip of the tip. No matter how deeply you penetrated you finally came to the void where the tip ended. To step into that void could only be a conscious act. It didn't happen accidentally. They nudged themselves toward the brink and then at the last possible moment held back. It was just as the Zen masters had described: "Those who hasten towards it dare not enter, fearing to hurtle down through the void with nothing to cling to or to stay their fall." Neither doubted that Enlightenment was something absolute and unmistakable. Sixty billion arhats couldn't be wrong. They would know it if it happened.

Increasingly they sensed they were trying to get back to a place they had already glimpsed. "Did you see something like a blue flash, so tiny it was almost not there, and then it vanished? I knew it was a messenger. I had the feeling it continued but we didn't have the strength of mind to follow it. It didn't disappear, we did." It became harder to attain states that had been easy in the beginning. They were mired in *samsara*. Convinced that the only way out was through each other, they kept doing the thing with the eyes. That way they could get rid of all the extraneous parts. Jack wouldn't be Jack anymore, he would just be what was mirrored in Jane's gaze. But what was mirrored *in* her eyes was already a mirror *of* her eyes. The reflections oscillated in a spiral pattern—like a cyclone, or one of those Gnostic aeons. From that swirling cloud a third presence was getting ready to be born, the etheric child of their minds.

Breath control was important because it kept the cadence steady. They learned to let air flow calmly in and out no matter what happened. It was like having a strong steady rhythm section so the sax could just float along on top of that without fear of falling. You had to tighten up in some areas to be loose in others. They worked at keeping their spines straight. They did head stands. They went without meat. They chanted. They hung a Tibetan tanka on the wall and sat in the lotus position staring at it for ever longer periods. On a good day the eleven heads of Avalokiteshvara, each perched on top of the other and culminating in a miniature Buddha head, would cease to be separate static forms and become a single pulsing shape. The eleven heads were really one continuously expanding head.

Tibet beckoned inevitably. Everything set it apart, even its height above sea level. Remote as it was, it had penetrated the West sufficiently to engender *Lost Horizon* and *Dr. Strange*: visions, however distorted, of an ultimate reality. The message had somehow gotten through. Tibet was simply the most powerful transmitter on the planet. If any magic at all survived, it had to be there, or in the adjacent mountains to which its lamas had fled from the Maoist army. That telepathic beacon, no matter how dwindled, was all that survived of the ancient mind arts. There, they could believe, people moved objects by thought power, made themselves invisible, sent humanoid mental projections on errands, transported themselves psychically from one peak to another.

Their arts were certainly magical enough. In the scroll paintings of gods and bodhisattvas, the ribbons of color and intricately looping lines were designed to set off multiple complex movements. The figures vanished, the colors reversed, the whole painting started revolving like a wheel. Each retinal reaction triggered another, opposite phase. Tibetan images refused to sit still, or to let the eye sit still. They forced the organism to participate in what it perceived. There were even projection mandalas where the center was blank and the mind of the viewer had to provide the god's image. Then there was the music, if it could be called music: it was more like a summons to the edge of being. The monks chanted so low that an echo was set off inside them, a pearl of sound, unvoiced yet penetrating everything. Gongs crashed to announce the end of the world: "Amid the vastness of flame, blazing like the fire of exploding universe, in the palace within the swirling black storm . . ."

One afternoon as they made love surrounded by mandalas, the hymn to Mahakala resonating in their ears, they found themselves spontaneously assuming the lotus position. It was like being plugged into a socket. While the structure of matter blackened and crashed all around them they held tight to each other, immobile but vibrating. He looked at her face and saw an open flame. They were not people anymore, they were just the raw material that made this vortex possible. Somewhere there was a friction of bone against bone. The rest was wind.

Often, when Jack and Jane thought afterward about the beings on the bed, it was to wonder where they had gone. That they had gone there could be no doubt. The hole in the air had closed. Access to the luminous wind tunnel was barred, and the very existence of the tunnel put in doubt. Their minds were full of characters and places that had not been there before. They woke from dreams of global melting to find a bare room with no hidden pouches, and dead sky behind its window

"I feel hollow all the time."

"It's like we died and never came back. On the street I can't believe how flat it is."

"I keep wanting that thing to happen. You know, *that* thing. There's nothing else worth looking at. What if this sluggish feeling never ends?"

"Don't look in my eyes again. It isn't there."

"But we saw it all. It went on forever."

"It did. But we don't."

"I keep thinking about *her*."

"Me too. Remember in high school we made up names for each other? She was Bad Girl, like in a fifties J.D. movie. It was a great show we put on. I guess all this time I secretly hoped we would find her in there somewhere. Like we would walk into a Himalayan valley where they restore souls, or at least get some kind of clear message, some token."

"I know. We'd live with the lamas and never have to be separated from anyone. And there would be no war because we'd pacify the planet with mind power."

"It's terrible not to be able to talk to her again."

"Well, we're not going to. The weird part is, we were going to bring her back to life and now we feel dead."

"Yeah, I don't suppose we're going to become enlightened after all."

"I wonder what it would have been like."

"Anyway, we had some fun."

"I guess so."

THE GREAT
FEAR

People got scared. They paced loft spaces for hours on end. With edgy determination they would grind their teeth or sit driving a jackknife into plywood. Hard to say what bothered them exactly. Nowadays nothing was separate from anything else. Pull on one coil and the whole damn thing yanked loose. "You know what it feels like? It feels like the end of time." "I'm not comfortable in the city anymore. Maybe I ought to get out to the country, only last time I was there I couldn't leave the house. Just could not get past that door." "Walk down the street, you can feel the spells being cast. That imbalance. The other day when I got high the woman next door started crying, I could hear her through the wall, and she just didn't stop, and after a while it really bothered me. Like she was fucking up the equilibrium of the universe somehow. Something was using her to get out into the city, into the world. What they used to call demons. Sneak into every crack they can find and then one day the scale tips and the world keels right over. You watch." "Something heavy is getting ready to come down, that much is for sure. I give the whole setup ten more years at the outside." "Watch what you say on that phone, it's probably tapped." "I'm getting very paranoid about all this fascism."

The killing and the talk of killing went on continuously now. Death, by assassination or suicide or police brutality or mistimed explosion of revolutionary matériel, had become a form of punctuation. Friends amazed themselves by making lists of the deaths. The only question was what could top what they had already witnessed. They felt ready for anything: plague, ice age, neo-Nazi putsch. Perhaps the recent cataclysms were part of a master plan to soften them up for the impending apocalypse—an event about which they grew more and more curious. If that was to be their fate, they might as well get on with it. It would, if nothing else, be an incomparable spectacle: the ultimate insider's screening, a movie never to be seen by anyone else, never to be remembered, an authentically one-of-a-kind experience.

Without fully realizing it, they had been in training all along for the end of the world. That was why they had aspired to become sages. What was a sage but someone so cooled-out as to be unperturbed even by nuclear dissolution? "I call that man enlightened who can gaze at the destruction of ten thousand worlds without flinching." Thanks to hallucinogenic magnification, they had each already witnessed more than one mini-apocalypse, and had acquired detachment in the process. "It's okay, I guess I'm just freaking out," someone would say as he watched his astral body melt into a compost of writhing insect life. Learning to live with the brain's manufactured horrors, to meditate calmly on the maggot swirl of molecules in the palm of the hand, was part of maturing. The world was an unstable swamp, a heaving Venusian bog. People were loose clusters of microorganisms that fleetingly coalesced within it. Any bodhisattva knew that.

The end of the world would be just another phenomenon. You had to let it happen, let it sweep over you. Surrender to the void and the Wrathful Deities would vanish as if they never had been—as, in fact, they never had been. The illusion popped like a bubble. You were free and clear and empty, so empty there wasn't even a "you" anymore. But in that case, who cared? Well, strictly speaking, there wasn't any caring anymore either. No address books, no souvenir snapshots, no names, no bodies, nothing left behind to rot: a universal absence hard and bright as diamond. The alternative was paranoia. Paranoia could be defined as a morbid longing for terror, a craving for personal memorabilia despite their unpleasant associations, a stubborn adherence to the discomforts of identity. "I don't want to relax! I'm afraid to relax!"

A paranoid person invariably ended up making a spectacle of himself. Anything like a shared wavelength repelled him. Incapable of trusting anyone, he fought any trend toward the merging of minds. He balked even at the most rudimentary grokking: "There's something wrong with this pot." Nothing did any good. It was in vain that the others sought him out in his hiding place: "Why don't you come back in the room with us, man? We'd all like to get down with you." He looked up and caught a diabolical gleam in the solicitous eyes. His friends were really the pod people from *Invasion of the Body Snatchers*. He would have to stay alert, fight off their influence, stick resolutely within his own boundaries. Meanwhile the others sat in a circle next door, savoring what was left of the oneness his presence had disrupted.

He was the sort of troublemaker who would harp on his property rights—"This is my room and I want you all to leave"—just as everyone else was realizing that nothing really belonged to anyone. He always held something back, short-circuiting potentially magical connections. If the rest managed to transcend temporality, he would be sure to bring them down by telephoning to find out the exact time. (In New York City this was accomplished by dialing

NERVOUS.) He clung with perverse pleasure to his wretched ego crises and professed not to understand what anyone else was talking about: "I think you make up this stuff about inner space, and then you all pretend you're talking about the same thing." "People who are out of touch with themselves always try to make other people feel alienated, don't they?"

But even if you considered yourself free from that elementary mistrust, you had to watch out for the paranoid undertow. Linger too long over any detail and it might you drag you down. It was imperative to be light on your feet, navigating among distortions with acrobatic ease. Other people would always try to suck you into their trip, so it helped to have your own trip ready to lay on them. In a constant silent duel the hipsters sniffed at each other's fear. You needed a sustaining framework, something on which you could peg your energies. Otherwise the chaos of the invisible world would tear you apart. You had to find your path and guard it with a combination of flexibility and wariness. To outsiders this might make you look like a shaman or a circus performer. New evolutionary conditions called for a new kind of personality.

A lady in a red cloak came to the door unbidden or three hours early, breathless with news of planetary influences. At night she moved around the city, jumping in and out of taxis, never arriving at any permanent destination. There was always one more message, one more urgent phone call. She was mistress of secret correspondences and karmic intersections. She brandished antique rings and spread Tarot cards out on cotton spreads, sighing in concern as she began to see what the fates had cooked up for her client. She transformed middle-class living rooms into arenas for magic: she analyzed dreams, interpreted physiognomies, demonstrated the traps in which people were caught and from which only she could free them.

She lived on nerve. She choreographed undercurrents. Somehow, as she shuttled in and out of other people's schedules, she made the crisscrossing cosmic trains run on time. Above all, she found channels for fears to flow through. If she didn't coax the latent threats and omens along, they might back up on her. At certain critical moments—they tended to hit at around four in the morning—the symbols she had been manipulating began to take their revenge. The stars closed in. The black magicians were tightening their invisible strings again. The weight of the Tarot card became unbearable. She left it face down, could not bring herself to turn it over. By the stark light of her low-rent kitchen she studied her eyes in a mirror made in Afghanistan. The splintered hallway and the all-night diner down the block were conspiring to shatter her balancing act.

So many were already dead or gone, fallen off roofs or shut up in Spanish prisons on charges of drug smuggling. Damage reports came in from both coasts, from London and Marrakesh, from the inland suburbs where some had retreated to nurse their wounds or unobtrusively fall apart. Even the poets were giving up, blowing out their brains in Ohio or crawling off to die in Nepal of neurological overload. Everybody complained about being tired. They couldn't face one more bust, one more abortion, one more suicide attempt.

Not that the madness in the outside world showed any signs of slowing down. The express would roar on, regardless of how many passengers decided to make a jump for it. The drugs—new and cruder varieties of psychedelic rotgut—would keep spreading, too, until the remotest villages were soaked in them. In small towns the police chief's son sold downers and homemade acid to junior high kids. The rednecks whose pool cues had once barred entrance to rural taverns were now more likely to be out back in the woods doing THC. Isolated subcultures sprang up, local religions taking as their text the lyrics of certain rock albums. One never knew.

Was this a Ten Years After town or a Yes town or a King Crimson town? The shared references evolved into dense private languages, nonspeakers of which were probably narcs. The priests of this community were the four who had a band going, played two nights a week at Rocky's Lounge, and interpolated their own material between cover versions of "Foxy Lady" and "Light My Fire." They had a long song describing landscapes on Mars that culminated in ten minutes of feedback effects. Afterward in the parking lot they talked about car crashes and ESP. "Do you see yourself more as a sender or a receiver?"

Information assumed increasingly peculiar shapes. The quality of news was measured by its grotesqueness. The only satisfying explanation of an event would be a reversal of all that had been previously believed. JFK, for instance, was not dead: he survived, a vegetable, in an underground chamber of Onassis' island. The great diplomat was a secret devil worshipper. In fact, the war was being run entirely by men who wore occult insignia under their tailored shirts. The real war between Russia and America was conducted psychically, by telekinetic armies held incommunicado in underground domes. Somewhere enmeshed in this global contest of minds were the rock stars, with their unimaginable wealth, their orgies of sadism, their power to influence millions through the subliminal vibrational patterns of their guitar solos. Or perhaps they in turn were enslaved by the sorcerers who kept them supplied with heroin in exchange for propagating messages of universal evil. Beneath the official news stories ran a current of hideous unprintable rumor.

The reality machine exemplified by *Time*, the *Times*, and CBS News had finally broken down. Fresh sources of instruction were opening up. One by one the graduates of half a decade's informational barrage were retiring into new kinds of cloisters and study groups. They were learning to erase a lifetime's accumulation of reactive feelings through Scientology, to achieve world unity by chanting "Nam myoho renge kyo," to find bliss through abstinence among the Hare Krishnas. These schools were more serious than the loose coalitions they had hitherto encountered. The groups had money; they had offices throughout the globe; they extended further than any one person could see, even though to the casual observer they were not visible at all. Their tiers and branches and intricately programed phases of induction described another kind of inner space. The enlistee entered the mandalic labyrinth not knowing what would happen. With excitement and dread he allowed himself to be ushered blindfolded through the stations of a second birth canal. There were rooms within rooms, doctrines concealed within doctrines, circles upon circles to be penetrated before reaching the innermost. Who would he have become by the time he got there?

If nothing else, he would speak a different language. The spiritual corporations were founded on vocabulary. Their specialized word lists differentiated inside from outside and ensured that the one could never be translated into the other. This speech was different in nature from those of the known world. Ordinary human languages used a variety of words—"table, *Tafel, tavola*"—to refer to the same basic objects. This one, on the contrary, took familiar words and applied them to unfamiliar feelings and experiences. "He's not on. I think I may be partway toward on." "When you're clear you'll get it." Such language was a continuous sexual act. Every sentence affirmed relationship. The initiate could not disconnect himself from what he spoke and thought with. Inside the compound, long and complicated discussions went back and forth. They were apparently describing the dimensions and properties of a vast fluid web. Outside, when he tried to recapitulate these dialogues for the benefit of old friends, the words disappeared.

The old friends looked about uneasily, afraid chiefly that they might begin to receive strange phone calls, that their names might be put on some list, that their lives would be invaded by the world of the secret societies. Lately there were so many people to be avoided: people with guns, people with mantras, people with special diets, people equipped with overbearing techniques of persuasion mastered in prolonged group sessions. It was increasingly hard to find anyone unaffiliated. Agents prowled around looking for recruits. The only way to tell them apart was that they always knew what to say and were able to make people feel awkward by interrupting or asking questions or sometimes just by remaining silent. Arguing was not only useless but potentially dangerous. "Those people are capable of anything. Don't even talk to them." "You can't hide from them. They wrote the book on weakness, they know just where to zero in." "I told them I didn't want to stay in the group, so they sent me to something they call a discipline officer who yelled at me for an hour about how I was a traitor, a coward, a CIA agent. Anyway, I left. Then the phone calls started. My boyfriend was getting them, too: don't see her, she's a bad influence, this is all going down on your record. My phone is unlisted now. But they're relentless, they never give up. I think maybe they're having me followed."

Another thing to look out for was people who were too relaxed. If a stranger seemed unaccountably trustworthy, if he exuded openness and ease, he was probably employing manipulative tricks. The word was passed on: Beware of seductive eyeball games, beware of loving vibrations. There was nothing that couldn't be faked. The greatest living teacher of meditation and celibacy had been secretly balling his female disciples for years, it turned out. Everybody's favorite underground newspaper was really a propaganda sheet for an authoritarian religion. The game had been about dominance from the start. There was a pornography of terror, a science of humiliation. The search for wisdom was governed by the dynamics of a biker movie. People afflicted with fear sought out the wise men who knew how to conquer fear. Now, having found them, they had to figure out how to conquer the fear of wise men.

A wise old man would wear a robe and carry a staff. He would preside with unwrinkled brow over pastoral rites: the keeper of the lore of the woods. He arose naturally from the resurrected springtime, part of its religion of the earth, its nostalgia for druidism, its celebration of equinox. Forest animals nestled at his feet and in his wake benign elves peeped from the shrubbery. But as the light faded, the elf eyes took on a demonic glint. Was that not the demon Hob, or the merciless goat-god? The ancient ecstasies brought an aftertaste of blood sacrifice and dismemberment. The animal was not to be brought harmlessly back to life: as he galloped in he bore the beast-world with him.

The blue-green magic of the natural world became discolored with the black-and-red color scheme of sorcery. The infusion of black magic was like the aftermath of a poisoning. Witch brews foamed and candles flickered while middle-class covens called on night and fire and the moon as a prelude to sex magic; *Rosemary's Baby* played the drive-ins; and on California beaches long-haired cultists gathered in the dark with murderous intent. It was bad acid made visible. At night in the psychedelic living rooms, how easy it had been for the kids to find Freudian gnomes curled in the corners of the body, or to mistake swirls of disorganized sensory data for visitations of Asmodeus or Beelzebub. Witchcraft and its accompanying tortures were woven into the language they spoke with, the pictures they looked at, the furniture and utensils they lived among. It was such recent history. As children they had thought it might be fun to go back there.

Now they sniffed real death in the remnants of their Halloween games. The Druids might well have come back, only it turned out they would slit your throat as soon as look at you. The occult imagination was surfacing, but not quite as advertised: instead of the gentle wizards sung by the Incredible String Band or the sublime Atlanteans of Donovan, its incarnations took the form of Charles Manson and his tribe of blood worshippers. Another Hitler cycle had clearly begun. The old exterminatory drive was stirring. What could be more terrible than the actualizing of long-buried thoughts? Under the influence of drugs and killing and sexual revolution, Amerika was making its Fantasyland real, willing into existence a roving cast of flagellants, assassins, and home-grown Rasputins. It was *Forbidden Planet* all over again: monsters from the Id enacting the secret wishes of the citizens who watched in horror.

The monsters cruised the parks and turnpikes of the country of desire. Their senses keen for prey, they navigated among the crevices of the new liberties. They committed slaughters in secluded driveways, and ten minutes later an exploitation movie was being made about them: *Savage Saviors* or *The Love Freaks*. The physiological details of their crimes crept into the reveries of gentle pot smokers, who started up sweating at the intrusion. Even more disturbing was the seductive cadence of Charles Manson's rapping, as reported in *Rolling Stone*. The voice didn't have to be imagined. It was the same voice whose afterecho had been the background music of the last five years, laid back and seductive and interminable: "Yeah, well, paranoia is just a kind of awareness, and awareness is just a form of love. Paranoia is the other side of love. Once you give in to paranoia it ceases to exist. . . . Total paranoia is total awareness. . . . The beautiful thing is that it's all there, everything's there in your mind. . . . I am you, and when you can admit that, you will be free. I am just a mirror."

It was hard not to listen, hard to shake off a creeping sense of complicity. In the era of contamination nothing stayed pure. The Beach Boys record to which one had been listening turned out to have lyrics by Charles Manson, and the Beatles' white album became retroactively polluted by having figured as the blueprint for Manson's killings. Any thought contained the seeds of evil. The mind would have to be sealed off altogether to avoid those killer brainwaves. Simply to walk down the street in Amerika was to bathe in murderousness. The lyrics of every rock song were being reconstructed into incitements to massacre somewhere inside the quiet drifter with the illegible face. He had been around, in and out of communes, cities, sects. People knew him as a long-haired loner who mostly liked to sit around picking out chords on his guitar. He had a notebook in which he wrote down little poems about loneliness and death. He waited for the right fragment of information to come along and wake him up to his task: the ritual cleansing, through violence, of a dying planet.

It did indeed appear to be dying. The panicked scurryings of the humans on its surface were only one indication. The more precise bulletins that started to come out confirmed what had already been intuited: The air is going. The sea is going. The poisons in your food are changing the color of the soil to match the sky's chemical violet. The nuclear waste is eating into the walls of its containers. The mechanism of birth itself fails. The eggs sicken. In the nests of the pelicans and the otters and the sea urchins the dying has already begun.

The people had done this to themselves. The centuries of self-hatred and sex-hatred and nature-hatred were culminating in the literal murder of the planet. In obedience to a blind god of hate, they hacked away at their own breeding ground. Too late to teach them: they had written their script and would follow it to the letter, all the way through to the horrors of the last act. They would die, and tear their stage down as they fell.

The fail-safe point had already been passed. A few lookouts scanned the blank horizon, but there was as yet no sign of the promised spacemen.

LAND'S END

Years had gone by. The war continued. The Atlanta airport was full of soldiers grounded by a thunderstorm. From among the duffel bags came talk of a night ambush. "We were on patrol, fuckers came from the side, wasted my main man." They slept wherever they could find space, in washrooms, on benches, in clusters by the check-in counter. The man and woman headed for California sat smoking and talking about almost anything except warfare. The soldiers made them self-conscious.

The plane didn't take off until morning. All the songs piped through the headphones were designed to elicit tears. Music had become uniformly plaintive and falsetto. It was like the sound track for a scene in which someone dies, or returns to his native land, or is suddenly and uselessly reminded of his native land.

Hollywood Boulevard proved more cramped than expected. The day was almost over. Members of an apocalyptic religious sect, emaciated and black-robed, were doing something outside a movie theater, something that involved silently shuffling back and forth and making their presence felt. Somebody was saying that the girls at orgies in Los Angeles were more enthusiastic than in other cities. The car moved through miles of low flat buildings. The plaster-white unfinished housing development bore the name of a Greek god and was modeled after the palaces in cut-rate Italian spectacles. Up in the canyon the rock musicians did yoga and heroin. Private saxophone music defined the interiors. There was a hole in the bedroom door where it had been smashed in anger a few nights earlier. Beyond the pool a dirt road led to the cliff's edge. The night city spread out like a special effect.

From the fast-food joint across the street, the kids of Hollywood High looked like extras in an American-International beach picture. "The girls on the beach are all within reach": as if one could simply have chosen for it to remain 1965, and for the whole world to be drenched in the unmodulated light of the International House of Pancakes. How could anything so color-saturated ever disappear?

The man and woman didn't want to linger in the city. They wanted to see a real place.

Their first ride, the one that took them to the edge of Los Angeles, was with a well-fed fortyish ad man. His silk shirt, explosive with floral patterning, stood out even through the windshield of his Porsche. Watery fusion music flowed from the tape deck. The ad man handed them a book without words: it contained nothing but page after page of mandalas embossed on achingly soft rice paper. "Isn't that the most beautiful thing you've ever seen? I just had to have one of these."

The next one, a girl who

rolled joints during stoplights, got them as far as Ventura. The back of her van, with a cot and a little bookshelf and a pile of R&B tapes, was so comfortable they didn't want to get out.

To the north it got tougher. They stood by the highway for hours until finally climbing into a beat-up truck full of laborers who passed a wine bottle back and forth. They stopped for gas after an hour or so. As he came around the corner after pissing he heard the guys in the van joking about maybe they should abduct the woman and leave him behind at the gas station. The idea seemed to be winning approval. The hippie who had come along for the ride, and on whom the man and woman had half-consciously relied for some kind of support, grinned brainlessly in the backseat. The station was an isolated outpost surrounded by woods and highway. It was beginning to feel like the prelude to one of those abrupt violent episodes with which the California papers routinely filled out their pages.

Eventually they managed to get abandoned by the roadside. They needed a place to stay. Night had already fallen. Through the trees came the thick smell of the ocean. In a clearing they met a local: "You can sleep on the beach if you want to." "Over there across the road?" "Sure. People sleep there sometimes. Of course, we did have a little trouble. Couple got killed by some slasher a few weeks ago. But there hasn't been anything like that since."

A mile farther along the road a campus rose up out of nowhere. It looked as if it had been built the day before. In its outlying areas it was more like a stop on a caravan route. A crowd of travelers milled around a fire where some soup was cooking. Recycled goods—flashlights, wrenches, paperback novels—were hawked along the fringes. In the yard behind a secondhand bookstore, cots and blankets and backpacks established an impromptu campground. "Can we sleep here?" "Sure, but you may have to fight for your woman." They ended up in a nearby motel. The drinking party next door—a floating assortment of teenage boys and girls—tapered off into moans and broken glass around the time the ocean light broke through. They walked outside. The campus buildings gleamed. A parade of surfers and beach girls, each impossibly tall and perfect, glided along in synchronized rhythm. Morning had broken upon another planet.

The highway got more and more crowded with hitchers. At every bend in the road there would be five or ten of them waiting, and at some exits the numbers swelled to tribal proportions. Conversation didn't amount to much. Nobody seemed too excited about anything. Mostly they talked about how the cops in Santa Maria were worse than the cops in Santa Barbara, and the cops in San Luis Obispo were the worst of all: "Don't try to stop there, just go straight on through." The gear and weaponry of the law glittered at every intersection. The man and woman who had come looking for the ocean found themselves trapped in a metallic network of badges and tollbooths and patrol cars.

There was the question of knowing where to alight, where to walk, where to enter. Any place in California was a grid of battle lines. A war of generations was being waged. "They ought to kill every one of them." Old and young eyed each other as if through the sights of shotguns.

Two guys in business suits bought them lunch. They talked about how they had met ten years earlier on acid in Golden Gate Park. Now one was a high-paid lawyer, the other a doctor. Afterward they broke out some Colombian Red, reminisced about Janis Joplin, and offered some advice: "Work? Why bother? If I were you I'd get on welfare. Let the system support you, man, what else is it good for?"Toward dusk they drove past Soledad. The blond boy driving the truck was talking about Hawaii. "You couldn't find a nicer place to live." The man and woman had confided that they were looking for a place to live. His account of the islands mesmerized them. They felt like children asking for a favorite bedtime story. This was what they had always wanted to hear: a tale of palm trees and waterfalls and coconuts, and old men gathering on a beach to fish and drink beer. "Man, I like to drink beer myself, but these Hawaiians bring one case apiece." The prison receded and vanished. They entered hill country. The road was lined with olive trees. The soft light persisted almost until they reached the marina.

The surfer driving at ninety miles an hour around the hairpin turns of Mount Tamalpais was as laconic and relaxed as anyone they had ever met. His speed exuded offhand magic. It paid peculiar homage to the mountain's splendors by reducing them to a blur of green and brown and blue: until, a last curve turned, the unblurrable ocean emerged. They began a giddy descent into paradise.

In an empty cove they stared and hummed all morning. They had nothing but themselves, their bodies by the roadside, their eyes and voices.

They walked along the highway for hours. There was nothing to do but take the next step.

That night they slept in the woods and woke up crawling with primeval beetles. At first light they staggered into the town, which turned out to be a post office and a bodega and a couple of fix-it shops. There was a whole crew waiting for rides. Finally a van came along big enough to take them all. The two pretty girls in black dresses who had been waiting with the rest now began to sing songs about Jesus, one of them shaking a tambourine for added effect. Nobody joined in or commented. The hymns continued all the way up the Sonoma coast.

In Mendocino the hippies blended more with the scenery. They would emerge unexpectedly, as if from behind camouflage, to offer tips on which way to walk or whether to enter the roadside diner: "I don't think you want to go in there. Really." They moved with the unobtrusive flexibility of hill people, appearing and vanishing in silence.

As they walked along the coast they came to a river. In the hot green light the land simply opened to let water through. They followed its course until a hippie in a van drove them to the nearest town. The street life in these parts had something of the river's fluidity. The town consisted mostly of men with beards and women with babies. The women, many of them pregnant, wore loose homemade dresses. The men wore overalls and work boots. The Laundromat was a collage of yogic symbols. On the main street motorcycles roared and weaved with a rhythm like Saturday night in a cowboy movie. It was the middle of the day. An old man spat on the sidewalk and turned away with an expression of impotent hatred. The town had been taken over. From alleys and porches the deposed residents surfaced momentarily, stared, stepped back into the shadows.

By the riverbank women were washing clothes. Farther on, a man sat meditating, his eyes fixed on the flow. "Where you folks bound for?" "We thought we might head back to Berkeley, look for a place to stay." "Ain't got no river in Berkeley." His eyes were back on the water.

On their way down the coast they stayed at a motel near where *The Birds* was filmed. The late movie was a Busby Berkeley musical starring Pat O'Brien. Its title—*The*

Garden of the Moon—gave it an exotic nobility. The black-and-white camera work was an unattainable tranquil sea surrounded by violent orange carpeting. Life in Pat O'Brien's music club was going considerably more smoothly than it was for the man and woman in the motel room. The geometrics of the floor show reminded them of a culture from which they had been exiled, an old way of life of which no trace was to be found either in the cities or along the banks of the great river. They had no desire to go in any particular direction. In the morning they continued heading south.

Dusty from the road they walked into a realtor's office in Berkeley. The realtor turned out to be a minister of some denomination they had never heard of. As for the apartment, it was a room crudely tacked onto a garage in the backyard of a run-down two-story house. Now all that remained was to get on the welfare rolls.

Framed portraits marked boundaries. In the welfare office there was a picture of Ronald Reagan. Malcolm X watched over the reading room of the local library. From the wall of the health food store Meher Baba stared down, like Stalin in an old Soviet movie.

On the kitchen wall of the commune next door were posted little mottoes about diet—"Nuts to you! And fruits too!"—and an ode to brown rice. The people rarely spoke to outsiders or raised their voices above a meditative mutter. Somebody's daughter—a child of four or five—wandered aimlessly around the yard while her elders did their "morning thing" and then, later on, their "afternoon thing." She communicated mostly with her eyes. None of the commune people paid any noticeable attention to her. She poked her head into the garage like an inquisitive cat and then crept noiselessly away.

Under the wooden bench in the

Laundromat he discovered a pornographic paperback about rubber fetishism. He had been reading *Remember Be Here Now* by Baba Ram Dass, a book which explained everything. He sat on the bench making an effort to be there now.

After a while they wanted some entertainment. The movie showing on Market Street was a long fantasy set in the nineteenth century. A woman sitting behind them repeated the same phrases for two and half hours: "Fathers fucking daughters, brothers fucking sisters, mothers fucking sons." The next feature was about tank warfare in North Africa.

Along Telegraph Avenue the sidewalk was thick with junkies and dealers, a twenty-four-hour drug market all the way to the university.

Everybody in San Francisco was talking about the past, constructing an oral history of the past ten years. The only ones talking about the future were the homosexuals who gathered in refurnished Victorian rooms to discuss political strategy. Their map of the next ten years sounded incredibly optimistic. Afterward they all went to a bar and danced for many hours to Wilson Pickett records.

One night a stranger paced back and forth on the walkway outside their garage window all night. "What's he *doing* there?" "I don't know, some California thing, go back to sleep." Toward dawn a rock smashed through the window. The walkway was empty. The man got dressed and strolled into the yard. He saw the guy—the usual gaunt long-haired guy with dead eyes—standing still and not doing anything at all. "Hi, how are you?" Unbroken silence. "You know, something kind of strange happened. We're staying in the room above the garage, you see, and sometime this morning a rock was thrown through our window. And we wondered—well, you were out here during the night and we wondered if you noticed anything unusual." Long pause: the eyes not accusatory, merely unresponsive. "As I was saying, we wondered—" "I didn't throw any rock through any window." The voice was calm and devoid of nuance. "I wasn't implying that you had. I simply meant that since you were out here you might have gotten a look—" "I didn't throw any rock through any window." "Well" (stepping back while the other remained immobile), "we just wondered. It was a little upsetting." The next pause was long enough to permit a quiet retreat. The stranger continued to stand by the gate, his eyes fixed on a remote imperceptible object.

Up and down the coast that summer the song hits seemed to tell a story: It's too late. What's going on? I scare myself.

Somebody on the beach on the far side of the mountain was handing out tabs of psilocybin. Eventually the sky and what lay under it appeared to be cunningly woven from billions of black dots. The reverse side of the things on the beach—the legs, the stray rocks, the pull, the girl's face, the scattered eyelashes—was a sheer black surface, slick as zinc. When he looked at the woman the oscillation was intolerably rapid: face to zinc to face to zinc.

The water ended. The land began. The light died with an air of indifference. After it was night they walked along a dirt road until they came to a bar. There was something wonderfully structured about the act of ordering a beer and paying for it and drinking it. He played the Marvin Gaye record repeatedly, wishing he might be that emotional but not quite getting there. The zinclike patina lingered on the world and its faces. They could not count how long they stayed there, except by the time they left the psilocybin had begun to wear off. A group of men at the next table were having an argument about the proper way to pronounce the word "bullshit." They tried out a few hundred ways, singly and in unison. Outside the sky was black. The man walked blindly along the road by the ocean. He had wandered off by himself. There was a stretch of flat grassy ground and he had never seen anything so tempting. He wanted only to fall toward the ground, and in falling to savor the weight of the fall, the chill of the night breeze, the texture of the ground as it came up to meet him. As if saying goodbye to sky and ocean he let himself go down. The earth approached, dark and welcoming. He decided that he had come to the end of his journey.